1944

WHAT A YEAR TO BE BORN!

Written by
Robin Bennett-Freebairn and Joe Toussaint

Published by Emersive
www.whatayeartobeborn.com

What happened in 1944? Most of us have a special affinity for the year we were born, but how much do we really know about it? This guide takes you through the highs and lows of an historic year near the end of World War Two. The colour-coded chapters unlock a wealth of information, bringing you closer to what life was like in this special year.

Contents

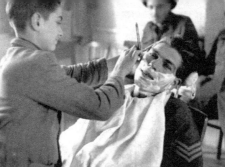

▶ Introduction

By 1944, the war was in its fifth year. Only a handful of nations declared themselves neutral and the conflict engulfed most of the globe. In the Casablanca Conference of 1943 the Allies, lead by Churchill and Roosevelt, called for the unconditional surrender of Nazi Germany. This meant that the hard part of the war could begin: fighting the Nazis on the ground in Europe. Town-by-town, street-by-street and house-by-house. Russia was making advances on the Eastern Front, Stalingrad had been relieved a year earlier. On the 27th January 1944, the siege of Leningrad was broken, to reveal over 1.5 million dead. Many German citizens, knowing that Soviet retribution would be uncompromising and brutal, took up arms for the first time even though they had no love for the Nazis. When on the 4th June 1940, Winston Churchill made his "We shall fight on the beaches" speech, he was referring to the defence of Britain. By 1944, the boot was on the other foot. On the 6th June 1944 British, American and Commonwealth forces landed on five beaches in Normandy. Resistance was mixed. The Americans met formidable firepower at the beach codenamed 'Omaha', but the British and Canadian forces at 'Sword' met minimal resistance. At home in London, which had got back to a semblance of normality since the Luftwaffe lost its ability to carry out sustained air raids, a new terror arrived as the Nazis launched their secret weapon, the V1 'Doodlebug' rocket. The first landed in London's Mile End at 4.35am on the 13th June 1944, killing six people and destroying a railway bridge. In the Far East, forces lead by America, but also involving troops from mainly Britain, India and Australia, were slowly closing in on the Japanese Empire island by island. The capture of New Guinea in April was of particular significance as it meant that all the major cities of Japan were now in range of land-based Allied bombers. Meanwhile, in America, the military were working on the most deadly weapon that the world had ever seen: the Atomic Bomb. The first reactor using heavy water and natural uranium, went critical on the 15th May 1944, meaning that a nuclear device was viable.

The year also saw the births of several stars who were amongst the last who could call themselves war babies: Diana Ross, Michael Douglas and Jerry Springer to name but a few. Although television had started in Britain as early as 1926, it was shut down during the war as it was thought that the signals would aid enemy bombers. Instead, people relied on the radio and the heavily censored Pathé News. It brought news of the war, often several weeks after events had happened. In film, *Casablanca* won the Best Picture Oscar and most cinemas chose to play it again. The British produced *Desert Victory*, a documentary using real-life footage of the North African Campaign, scooped the award for best documentary. Little sport was played in Britain, although a Football League War Cup was set up. Aston Villa won the Northern final and Charlton Athletic the Southern. The score in the National final was tied at 1-1, but due to bombing threats a replay was not held. The trophy was shared, an event that had not happened before nor since.

The Daily Headlines

No: 1415

Price: Twopence

Evening Edition

Tuesday, June 6, 1944

D-DAY NORMANDY LANDINGS BEGIN WITH BRITISH, US AND CANADIAN TROOPS INVOLVED

The Daily Headlines

Price: Twopence

Tuesday, June 13, 1944

No: 1420

Evening Edition

FIRST V-1 FLYING BOMBS STRIKE MILE END IN LONDON TERRIFYING LOCAL RESIDENTS

The Daily Headlines

Price: Twopence

Tuesday, September 19, 1944

No: 1502

Evening Edition

DAMBUSTERS HERO, GUY GIBSON, IS KILLED IN PLANE CRASH DURING BOMBING RAID

The Daily Headlines

No: 1544

Evening Edition

Price: Twopence

Saturday, October 14, 1944

THE 'DESERT FOX', ERWIN ROMMEL, COMMITS SUICIDE BY CYANIDE PILL AHEAD OF TRIAL FOR HIGH TREASON

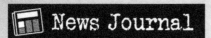
Jan 1st   The Luftwaffe launch Operation Bodenplatte (Baseplate), an
            attempt to deplete Allied air strength in the Low Countries.
            Whilst the attack goes undetected by Allied Intelligence, the
            German Air force suffers its largest single-day loss of the war.

Jan 2nd   A Tree Grows in Brooklyn, by Betty Smith, tops the New York Times
            Fiction Bestseller list.

Jan 11th   Franklin D. Roosevelt issues the State of the Union Address to
            Congress. In it he proposes a Second Bill of Rights, guaranteeing
            such things as medical care, housing and education.

Jan 11th   Alfred Hitchcock's film Lifeboat, starring Tallulah Bankhead and
            William Bendix, is released.

Jan 12th   Prime Minister Winston Churchill and the leader of the Free
            French, Charles De Gaulle, begin a two-day conference in Morocco
            to discuss the French role in the proposed D-Day Landings.

Jan 17th   The battle of Monte Cassino begins.

Jan 17th   A diplomatic incident occurs when the Soviet newspaper Pravda
            publishes an erroneous report claiming that representatives from
            Britain and Germany have met on the Iberian Peninsula to discuss
            making a separate peace. The British Foreign Office quickly
            quashes the rumour in an official letter to the Soviet government.

Jan 18th   The Siege of Leningrad, which began on 8th September 1941, is
            finally broken when the Red Army opens up a corridor south of
            Lake Ladoga.

Jan 19th   The RAF conduct their heaviest raid on Berlin yet, dropping 2,300
            tons of bombs in just over half an hour.

Jan 20th   The Battle of Anzio, Italy begins. The Allied objective is to
            outflank German forces and open up a pathway to Rome.

Jan 24th   The British hospital ship St. David is bombed and sinks off Anzio,
            south of Rome, despite being well-marked and lit in accordance
            with laws of war. 96 of the 229 on-board perish.

Jan 25th   The Red Army lifts the Siege of Leningrad and reveals the full
            horror of what has taken place there. A million and a half
            civilians have died and countless others are close to starvation.

Jan 30th   Adolph Hitler gives a radio address on the eleventh anniversary of the Nazis coming to power. In it he barely mentions the war, instead he talks about Germany being Europe's bulwark against Communism.

Feb 1st   Unpopular clothing restrictions are lifted in Britain after two years. These had imposed limits on the number of pockets, pleats and buttons that could be incorporated into clothing.

Feb 9th   The Bishop of Chichester, George Bell, opens a debate in the House of Lords about the legitimacy of bombing European cities. In it he states "There must be a fair balance between the means employed and the purpose achieved. To obliterate a whole town because certain portions contain military and industrial establishments is to reject the balance."

Feb 11th   Father Claude H. Heithaus delivers a sermon at Saint Louis University, Missouri denouncing racial prejudice. He is then forcibly removed from the State.

Feb 12th   The German steamboat Oria sinks in a storm whilst carrying over 4,000 Italian prisoners of war between Rhodes and Piraeus. It is one of the biggest losses of life in the history of the Mediterranean.

Feb 15th   The office of Otto Hahn, who has been working on the German nuclear programme, takes a direct hit in an Allied bombing raid. It is the intended target. Hahn is uninjured.

Feb 16th   The Lord Chancellor, John Simon, makes a speech in the House of Lords defending the British bombing campaign. Referring specifically to the monastery at Monte Cassino, he says that most of the buildings there dated from the nineteenth century and that the most valuable art treasures and manuscripts had been moved elsewhere.

Feb 19th   187 planes of the Luftwaffe bomb London. It is the heaviest bombing of the capital since May 1941.

Feb 22nd   French Surrealist poet and resistance fighter Robert Desnos is arrested in Paris and sent to Auschwitz concentration camp.

Feb 22nd   The British oil tanker British Chivalry is sunk by Japanese submarine I-37 in the Indian Ocean. I-37 then circles the sinking vessel and shoots the survivors. The submarine's commander Nakagawa Hajime is marked out as a war criminal.

Feb 23rd   The 'Father of the Plastics Industry' and inventor of Bakelite, Leo Baekeland, dies in New York aged 80.

Feb 25th   Operation 'Big Week', a concerted Allied bombing effort to deplete the German aviation industry, ends with heavy British and US losses. However, air superiority over the Luftwaffe is achieved.

Feb 28th   German aviator Hanna Reitsch visits Hitler to be awarded her second Iron Cross medal. During the ceremony she suggests that Hitler forms a suicide squad to fly specially adapted V-1 rockets. She even puts herself forward as a potential pilot. Hitler rejects the idea.

Mar 1st   In a bombing raid on Rome, six bombs from an RAF plane land close to the Vatican wall, killing a workman and injuring others.

Mar 2nd   At the 16th Academy Awards ceremony held in Grauman's Chinese Theater on Hollywood Boulevard, Casablanca wins Best picture.

Mar 3rd   In Rome, a protest of women demanding the release of their husbands detained by German forces, ends in tragedy. Seven months pregnant Teresa Gullace is killed by a soldier while trying to pass a sandwich to her husband.

Mar 6th   American heavy bombers launch their first ever full-scale daylight raid on Berlin.

Mar 8th   In Parliament, the Government announces plans to build 300,000 new homes after the war.

Mar 11th   In Paris, police stumble across the remains of at least 10 bodies at the home of Dr. Marcel Petoit. The serial killing doctor is out at the time and evades capture.

Mar 17th   Mount Vesuvius erupts killing 26 civilians, destroying 88 American aircraft and displacing 12,000 Italians.

Mar 24th   A 'Great Escape' takes place overnight into the 25th, when 76 RAF prisoners escape from Stalag Luft III via painstakingly constructed tunnels. Only 3 men, Norwegians Per Bergsland and Jens Müller and Dutchman Bram Van Der Stok, fully escape.

Mar 24th   A 'Lucky Escape' takes place in Germany when RAF pilot Nicholas Alkemade survives a fall of 18,000ft without a parachute when his

Lancaster bomber is shot down. Pine trees and snow break his fall

Mar 28th   In Parliament, MPs vote to pay women teachers the same as their male colleagues.

Apr 1st   A trip to the seaside is off for many as the government bans visitors from going within ten miles of the coast between Land's End and The Wash. Something's brewing.

Apr 4th   A South African Air Force de Havilland Mosquito surveillance plane takes photographs of Auschwitz Concentration Camp.

Apr 14th   800 people are killed in Bombay when the British freighter Fort Stikine catches fire causing two huge explosions.

Apr 15th   Giovanni Gentile, described by Mussolini as the "Philosopher of Fascism", is shot dead by anti-Fascist Partisans.

Apr 21st   Charles de Gaulle issues a decree from his base in Algiers awarding French women the vote.

Apr 22nd   A two-day meeting between Hitler and deposed Italian Dictator Mussolini takes place near Salzburg. The once animated "Duce" is reportedly a shadow of his former self.

Apr 27th   The British Government bans all travel abroad.

Apr 30th   The first of the proposed 300,000 pre-fabricated new build homes goes on show at the Tate Gallery in London.

May 5th   After nearly two years of house arrest at the Aga Khan's Palace in Pune, Mahatma Gandhi is released on medical grounds.

May 13th   Near Cassino in Italy, British Army Captain Richard Wakeford kills a number of enemy soldiers and takes 20 prisoners, armed only with a revolver.

May 14th   Wakeford is at it again. Today he leads a successful attack on an enemy hill position, in spite of being injured in the face, arms and legs. Can you win two Victoria Crosses on consecutive days?

May 14th   Vichy radio reports that French cardinals have appealed to the Roman Catholic clergy in Britain and the United States to use their

influence to ensure that the French civilian population as well as towns, works of art and churches be spared from Allied bombing as much as possible.

May 18th   The 123-day Battle of Monte Cassino comes to an end when German forces surrender their positions.

May 22nd   The week's edition of Life magazine publishes a picture of a young American woman with a Japanese skull which has been sent to her by her boyfriend serving in the Far East. The Army's bureau of Public Relations to inform US Publishers that "the publication of such stories would be likely to encourage the enemy to take reprisals against American dead and prisoners of war."

May 23rd   98% of the Icelandic electorate vote to break away from Denmark.

May 24th   Allied forces pierce the imaginatively named Hitler Line, a defensive position in Italy. It is immediately renamed the Senger Line after Fridolin von Senger, a German commander at the Battle of Monte Cassino.

May 30th   Princess Charlotte of Monaco abdicates her rights to the throne in favour of her son Prince Rainier.

Jun 1st   The BBC broadcasts a coded message based on the poem Chanson d'automne ("Autumn Song"), by Paul-Marie Verlaine. The recital lets the Resistance know that an Allied invasion is imminent.

Jun 2nd   In Soham, Cambridgeshire, a freight train carrying munitions explodes and kills two people.

Jun 4th   Rome falls to the Allies. American tanks roll along the Appian Way. Retreating German forces have ignored Hitler's order to blow up the bridges over the Tiber so these historic city sites are left intact.

Jun 5th   On the advice of RAF meteorologist James Stagg, the proposed D-Day Landings are postponed because of bad weather in the Channel

Jun 5th   The D-Day naval deception begins. Allied ships and aircraft make movements towards Calais in order to convince the Germans that the landings will take place there.

Jun 6ᵗʰ   If, in Churchill's words of 1942, that the victory at El Alamein was the "End of the Beginning", the D-Day landings must surely signify the "Beginning of the End." Allied forces land on five beaches in Normandy. President Roosevelt's address to the nation takes the form of a prayer: "Almighty God: Our sons, pride of our Nation, this day have set upon a mighty endeavour, a struggle to preserve our Republic, our religion, and our civilisation, and to set free a suffering humanity. Lead them straight and true; give strength to their arms, stoutness to their hearts, steadfastness in their faith."

Jun 7ᵗʰ   Actress Judy Garland divorces her husband, songwriter David Rose, citing general cruelty.

Jun 8ᵗʰ   The war film Days of Glory is released. It marks the screen debut of a handsome young man named Gregory Peck.

Jun 13ᵗʰ   Germany launches the first V-1 flying bombs at England. One of ten fired lands on Grove Road in Mile End killing three and damaging a railway bridge. Terror has returned to the skies of London.

Jun 14ᵗʰ   An RAF Mosquito records the first successful downing of a V-1 rocket over the English Channel

Jun 18ᵗʰ   A V-1 rockets hits the Wellington Barracks in Central London killing 121 people.

Jun 20ᵗʰ   The Battle of the Philippine Sea ends in American victory. Japanese forces have been routed. Their total losses are two aircraft carriers, two oil supply boats and around 600 aircraft.

Jun 20ᵗʰ   A German-made V-2 rocket becomes the first man-made object in space during a test launch.

Jun 24ᵗʰ   The widely acclaimed poet Ern Malley is revealed as a hoax in the Adelaide Mail The poet who apparently died a complete unknown turns out to be the creation of satirists James McAuley and Harold Stewart, who sought to highlight the pretentiousness of Modernist poetry. Much of the literary establishment were taken in.

Jun 30ᵗʰ   President Roosevelt signs a bill providing independence for the Philippines once Japanese forces are removed from the island group.

Jun 30ᵗʰ   Bush House, the headquarters of BBC's World Service, takes a direct hit from a flying bomb.

Jul 1st   A German counter-attack, aimed at dislodging British forces fails.
When Commander von Rundstedt phones Berlin to report the
failure, Chief-of-Staff Keite asks "What shall we do?" Rundstedt
replies, "Make peace, you fools! What else can you do?"

Jul 2nd   For his outburst the previous day Commander von Rundstedt is
replaced.

Jul 4th   To celebrate Independence Day, American General Omar Bradley
orders all artillery units to open fire on the German lines at
noon on the dot. Some units fire red, white and blue smoke shells.
Morale is greatly boosted.

Jul 6th   Winston Churchill gives a speech to the House of Commons about
the impact of the V-1 bombing campaign. He reveals that
government figures show that 2,752 British people have been
killed and approximately 8,000 injured.

Jul 9th   The Pacific War's D-Day, the Battle of Saipan, ends in victory for
America over Japanese Imperial Forces.

Jun 13th   The Sir John Soane designed Dulwich Picture Gallery takes a
direct hit. Some artworks are damaged, but thankfully the main
collection had been moved to an underground site in Wales.

Jul 17th   A munitions explosion in Port Chicago, California, leaves 320
people dead.

Jul 20th   A plot to assassinate Hitler is thwarted when a case containing a
bomb is unwittingly moved. The Fuhrer escapes with cuts and
bruises and a perforated eardrum.

Jul 20th   At 6:30pm a radio broadcast announces that Hitler is alive. A coup
attempt has failed. Retribution is swift and brutal

Jul 20th   Franklin D. Roosevelt accepts the Democratic nomination for
President. He states his decision to accept the nomination is "based
solely on a sense of obligation to serve if called upon to do so by
the people of the United States."

Jul 21st   Perhaps unable to sleep, at 1 a.m., Hitler gives a speech over the
radio to prove to the German people that he is still alive. He
declares that the conspirators will be "exterminated quite
mercilessly."

Aug 1st Scientists in Britain announce that DDT has been found to be an effective insecticide.

Aug 2nd Germany launches 316 V-1 rockets at London. More than 100 reach the capital, with one hitting Tower Bridge. Of more strategic concern are the ones that hit armaments factories on the outskirts of the city.

Aug 4th The family of Anne Frank are discovered in an attic in Amsterdam. They are detained and transported. Her father, who is out at the time, evades capture.

Aug 12th Joseph P. Kennedy Jr., eldest son of Joseph P. Kennedy Sr. and brother of John F. Kennedy, dies when his Liberator plane explodes over Blythburgh, Suffolk.

Aug 18th The Red Cross enter Drancy internment camp after it had been abandoned by the Nazis. They find around 500, mainly Jewish, survivors.

Aug 19th The Battle for Paris begins. Emboldened, the French Resistance begin a campaign of sniper attacks against the increasingly nervous and demoralised German forces.

Aug 25th The Battle for Paris ends when the German commander von Choltitz surrenders. Mid-afternoon Charles de Gaulle arrives in the city to walk among cheering crowds. He then delivers a stirring speech at the Hotel da Ville. Cries of "liberté" ring out around the city. Some women, suspected of fraternising with the enemy, have their heads shaved to humiliate them. Other collaborators are simply killed.

Aug 25th Romania switches sides and declares war on Germany.

Sep 1st Frank Capra's dark comedy Arsenic and Old Lace, starring Cary Grant, opens at The Strand Theatre in New York.

Sep 2nd Finland severs all relations with Nazi Germany and orders all German nationals to leave the country.

Sep 5th Sweden, who have given refugee status to Danish Jews, says it will ban entry to any Nazi fleeing from Germany.

Sep 6th Ypres in Belgium, the site of two major battles in the First World war, is liberated from occupying German forces by the Polish Army.

Sep 8th — The first V-2 flying bomb to land in Britain destroys 11 houses in Staveley Road, Chiswick, London. It kills 3 people and injures 22.

Sep 11th — US forces cross the border into Nazi Germany for the first time. A seven person reconnaissance mission crosses the border with Luxembourg and returns after encountering no resistance.

Sep 13th — British spy and Indian Princess Noor Inayat Kahn is captured in France by the Nazis and executed.

Sep 25th — Operation Market Garden, an attempt by the allies to cross the Rhine, ends in defeat. It is simply a bridge too far.

Sep 28th — Winston Churchill announces the formation of a Jewish Brigade. He states: "It seems to me indeed appropriate that a special Jewish unit of that race which has suffered indescribable torment from the Nazis should be represented as a distinct formation among the forces gathered for their final overthrow."

Oct 2nd — An uprising in the Warsaw Ghetto is brutally suppressed by Nazi occupation forces.

Oct 2nd — Poet Dylan Thomas is due to be best man at the wedding of his friend and fellow poet Vernon Watkins, but fails to turn up.

Oct 5th — Nazi Germany's propagandist-in-chief, Joseph Goebbels, cannot sugar-coat the news that food rations are to be reduced. Most Germans shrug their shoulders as Germany has virtually no means of importing food. Supplies in the shops are running low.

Oct 7th — In Italy, V division of the Eighth Army crosses the Rubicon. Like Julius Caesar before them, it marks a point of no return.

Oct 9th — At the Fourth Moscow Conference, Britain, Russia and the USA discuss the composition of Post-War Europe. Churchill proposes different spheres of influence, written on a scrap of paper, much to the delight of Stalin. Churchill comments: "Might it not be thought rather cynical if it seemed we had disposed of such issues, so fateful to millions of people, in such an offhand manner? Let us burn the paper." Stalin, However, counsels to save it.

Oct 12th — Canadian Polar explorer Henry Larson reaches Vancouver after sailing from Halifax, Nova Scotia via the North West Passage in just 86 days.

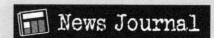
Oct 14th   Germany's greatest wartime general, Erwin Rommel, chooses to kill himself rather than face reprisals for his alleged part in the 20th July plot to assassinate Hitler. The German people are told that he died heroically in battle.

Oct 18th   Rommel is given a State Funeral in Ulm, a city on the Danube. Hitler does not attend, maybe there are too many generals present.

Oct 19th   The Cuba-Florida Hurricane makes landfall in Florida. It causes widespread damage and leaves over 300 dead.

Oct 20th   The Philippines Campaign commences. In a radio broadcast, General Douglas MacArthur begins: "This is the Voice of Freedom, General MacArthur speaking. People of the Philippines: I have returned." Thus referencing a speech he made in March 1942, when the US retreated from the islands.

Oct 21st   A Japanese aircraft laden with explosives crashes into the foremast of the ship HMAS Australia, in what is thought to be the first Kamikaze attack.

Oct 26th   Princess Beatrice, youngest daughter of Queen Victoria and mother of Louis Mountbatten, dies aged 87.

Oct 31st   Serial killer Dr. Marcel Petiot is arrested at a Paris Metro station where he is recognised in spite of growing a beard.

Nov 1st   The American destroyer Abner Read is sunk off the coast of the Philippines in a Kamikaze attack.

Nov 3rd   The Japanese begin their Fu-Go (Fire Balloon) campaign against mainland USA. These inaccurate weapons, which rely on the wind, cause little damage but much panic.

Nov 6th   The world's largest penicillin factory begins production in Liverpool.

Nov 12th   After several unsuccessful attempts, Bomber Command finally sinks the German flagship battleship, namely the Bismark-class Tirpiz.

Nov 14th   Jewish-Italian scientist Primo Levi and Auschwitz inmate, passes a chemistry exam in German, a language he doesn't speak. It secures him a menial job at the rubber plant in the concentration camp, increasing his chances of survival from zero to one-percent.

Nov 20th — Hitler leaves his Eastern Front headquarters, the Wolfsschanze, as the Red Army closes in. The hunter has now become the prey.

Nov 22nd — Lawrence Olivier's reworking of Shakespeare's Henry V opens in London. Olivier both directs and stars in the film.

Dec 3rd — The Home Guard, informally known as Dad's Army, is officially stood down as the threat of invasion has gone. Maybe someone will make a hard-hitting drama series about them in the future?

Dec 6th — In Britain the process of returning evacuees to towns and cities unaffected by V-rocket attacks begins.

Dec 13th — Russian painter and art theorist Wassily Kandinsky dies, aged 77.

Dec 15th — 97 Italian prisoners of war escape from a camp at Doonfoot in Scotland via a tunnel they had been constructing for months. They escape with no plans, more than 1500 miles from home and with their homeland divided and in tatters. They are soon rounded up.

Dec 18th — In Paris, the newspaper Le Temps is no more. Its reputation has been sullied by the Occupation. It is replaced by Le Monde, who even move into their old offices.

Dec 20th — Dwight D. Eisenhower is made a five-star general of the American Army.

Dec 23rd — Don't Fence Me In, by Bing Crosby and the Andrews Sisters, is announced as the Christmas number one in America.

Dec 24th — President Franklin D. Roosevelt addresses America and the World:

"It is not easy to say 'Merry Christmas' to you, my fellow Americans, in this time of destructive war. Nor can I say 'Merry Christmas' lightly tonight to our armed forces at their battle stations all over the world, or to our allies who fight by their side. Here at home, we will celebrate this Christmas Day in our traditional American way because of its deep spiritual meaning to us; because the teachings of Christ are fundamental in our lives; and because we want our youngest generation to grow up knowing the significance of this tradition and the story of the coming of the immortal Prince of Peace and Good Will. But, in perhaps every home in the United States, sad and anxious thoughts will be continually with the millions of our loved ones who are suffering hardships and misery, and who are risking their very lives to preserve for us and for all mankind the fruits of His teachings and the foundations of civilisation itself. The Christmas spirit lives tonight in the bitter cold of the front lines in Europe and in the heat of the jungles and swamps of Burma and the Pacific islands. Even the roar of our bombers and fighters in the air and the guns of our ships at sea will not drown out the messages of Christmas which come to the hearts of our fighting men. The thoughts of these men tonight will turn to us here at home around our Christmas trees, surrounded by our children and grandchildren and their Christmas stockings and gifts; just as our own thoughts go out to them, tonight and every night, in their distant places."

Dec 25th   Pope Pius XII delivers his Christmas Message. In it he states: "But when the goodness and kindness of God our Saviour appeared" (St. Paul's Epistle to Titus, Chap. 3, 4th verse).

"For the sixth time since the opening of the dreadful war, the Christmas liturgy again hails with these words redolent of peaceful serenity, the coming into our midst of God, our Saviour. Heads that were bowed lift again serenely, for Christmas is the feast of human dignity. The wonderful exchange by which the Creator of the human race, taking a living body, deigned to be born of a virgin, and by His coming bestowed on us His divinity. For alas, for the sixth time, the Christmas dawn breaks again on battlefields spreading ever wider, on graveyards where are gathered the remains of victims in ever-increasing numbers, on desert lands where a few tottering towers tell with silent pathos the story of cities once flourishing and prosperous, and where bells fallen or carried off no longer awaken the inhabitants with their jubilant Christmas chimes."

Dec 26th   The Glass Menagerie by Tennessee Williams has its first outing in Chicago.

Dec 27th   David Lloyd George, British Prime Minister during World War I, announces his retirement from Parliament.

Dec 27th   The 50-day Siege of Budapest by Soviet and Romanian forces begins.

Dec 31st   In a major victory for Filipino and American forces, the Battle of Leyte Island sees forces led by Douglas MacArthur triumph over Japanese forces, most of whom fight to the death. Of the 70,000 strong Japanese Imperial Army 65,000 are killed.

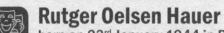

Rutger Oelsen Hauer
born on 23rd January 1944 in Breukelen, Utrecht, Netherlands

Rutger Hauer was the son of drama teachers Arend and Teunke, and grew up in Amsterdam. At the age of 15, he ran off to sea and spent a year scrubbing decks aboard a freighter. Returning home, he worked as an electrician and a carpenter for three years while attending acting classes at night school. He went on to join an experimental troupe, where he remained for five years before he was cast in the lead role in the very successful 1969 television series *Floris*, a Dutch Ivanhoe-like medieval action drama. Hauer's career changed course when director Paul Verhoeven cast him as the lead in *Turkish Delight* (1973). The movie found box-office favour abroad as well as at home, and within two years, its star was invited to make his English-language debut in the British film *The Wilby Conspiracy* (1975). Hauer made his American debut in the Sylvester Stallone vehicle *Nighthawks* (1981), cast as a psychopathic and cold-blooded terrorist named 'Wolfgar' (after a character in the Old English poem Beowulf). The following year, he appeared in arguably his most famous and acclaimed role as the eccentric, violent, yet sympathetic replicant Roy Batty in Ridley Scott's 1982 sci-fi thriller, *Blade Runner*. He was often cast in a villainous or evil role including *The Hitcher* (1986), *Buffy the Vampire Slayer* (1992), *Batman Begins* (2005) and *Sin City* (2005). Hauer was knighted in the Netherlands in 2013. He was also a passionate environmentalist. During the late 1980s and early 1990s, Hauer became well known to the British mainstream for a series of Guinness commercials where he is clad in black. He was a non-drinker and had to spit it out after each take.

Alice Malsenior Tallulah-Kate Walker
born on 9th February 1944 in Eatonton, Georgia, USA

Alice was the youngest daughter of sharecroppers. She grew up poor, with her mother working as a maid to help support the family's eight children. Living in the racially divided South, Walker displayed a bright mind at her segregated schools, graduating from high school as class valedictorian. With the help of a scholarship, Walker was able to attend Spelman College in Atlanta. After college, she worked as a social worker, teacher and lecturer and became active in the Civil Rights Movement fighting for equality for all African Americans. Walker's experiences informed her first collection of poetry, *Once* (1968). Better known now as a novelist, Walker showed her talents for storytelling in her debut novel, *The Third Life of Grange Copeland* (1970). In 1982, her career as a writer took off with the publication of her third novel, *The Color Purple*. Set in the early 1900s, the novel explores the female African American experience through the life and struggles of its narrator, Celie. She suffers terrible abuse at the hands of her father and husband. The compelling work won Walker both the Pulitzer Prize for Fiction and the National Book Award for Fiction in 1983. In 1985, Walker's story made it to the big screen: Spielberg directed *The Color Purple*, which starred Whoopi Goldberg as Celie, as well as Oprah Winfrey and Danny Glover. Like the novel, the movie was a critical success.

Quote: "I think it pisses God off if you walk by the color purple in a field somewhere and don't notice it."

 ### Gerald Norman 'Jerry' Springer
born on 13th February 1944 in London, UK

Springer was most famous for *The Jerry Springer Show*, a daytime talk show that featured highly contentious topics and outrageous guest behaviour. Springer's family relocated from London to New York when he was five. In 1965, he graduated from Tulane University with a degree in politics. He later took a law degree at a School of Law in Chicago. Following graduation, he worked on the presidential campaign of Robert F. Kennedy. In the early 1970s, he embarked on his own political career in Ohio, serving on the Cincinnati City Council. Springer was liberal by leaning, but he managed to secure the mayoralty of the conservative city in 1977. In 1982, he made an unsuccessful attempt for the Democratic nomination for governor of Ohio. He then turned his attention to television. He started off as a reporter for a local television station and rose to be anchor, a role that won him seven Emmy awards. In 1991, he branched out into talk shows with the debut of *The Jerry Springer Show*. Initially the programme centred on politics, but ratings were poor. Then Springer hit on a formula that would propel him to fame and notoriety in equal measure. By the mid-1990s the show was know for its controversial topics, fights and scantily clad guests. The King of Trash TV had truly arrived. The show ran from 1991 to 2018 across 27 seasons and nearly 5,000 episodes. He then went on to host an arbitration-based reality court show, *Judge Jerry*, from 2019 to 2022.

Springer was born deep underground in Highgate Tube Station on London's Northern Line, where his mother was sheltering from an air raid.

Roger Harry Daltrey CBE
born on 1st March 1944 in London, UK

Roger Daltrey is noted as a founder of the legendary rock band The Who. After leaving London's Acton County Grammar School in 1963, he formed a skiffle band called The Detours, then displayed an early genius by putting together unusual elements into a world-class rock band. These included Daltrey on vocals, John Entwistle on bass and Pete Townsend on lead guitar. In 1965, they added drummer Keith Moon. The band was remarkable for the synthesis of personalities: Townsend's art-school sensibilities, Daltrey's down-to-earth interpretations and Entwistle's and Moon's skill as performers. They were first noted for deafening shows and for smashing their instruments in ferocious displays of auto-destructive art, but they went on to considerable chart success through original songs written by Townsend and the more humour-oriented Entwistle. Daltrey's energy and stage presence established The Who at the monumental Monterey Pop, Woodstock and Isle of Wight music festivals, and his instincts for production carved their path through the era of stadium rock. He released his first solo album in 1973, and followed that with a number of solo chart successes. He also established a stage and offbeat film career after starring in the movie of *Tommy* (1975). He pursued films after the death of drummer Moon, and turned to production with the drama *McVicar* (1980).

Both he and former band mate Pete Townsend now wear hearing aids. He attributes this to years of exposure to the ear-splitting volume of the band's amplification systems.

Dame Kiri Jeanette Claire Te Kanawa ONZ DBE CH
born on 6th March 1944 in Gisborne, New Zealand

As a five-week-old infant, the then Claire Mary Teresa Rawstron was adopted by Tom and Nell Te Kanawa and given the name Kiri. Tom, like her biological father, was Maori and his wife, like Kiri's biological mother, was of Irish descent. Kiri attended a Roman Catholic girls' college in Auckland where one of the nuns was a well-known singing teacher. After leaving school, she won various singing competitions in New Zealand and Australia. In 1966, after a period as a popular singer and recording artist, she became a student at the London Opera Centre. As a soprano, she rose to international fame in a series of concerts at the Royal Opera House in Covent Garden. Her first big success was as the Countess in Mozart's *The Marriage of Figaro* (1971). That was followed by a run of Mozart operas and, among others, a production of Puccini's *La Bohème* in which she sang Mimi. Her debut at New York's Metropolitan Opera (1974) as Desdemona in Verdi's *Otello* was widely acclaimed. In 1981, she sang at the wedding of the then Prince Charles and Lady Diana Spencer. Her rendering of *Handel's Let The Bright Seraphim* reached a worldwide television audience of more than 600 million. She was created a Dame Commander of the Order of the British empire (DBE) in 1982. In January 2010, Dame Kiri and BBC Radio 2 launched a competition to find a gifted opera singer of the future. The winner, Shuna Scott, got to sing alongside Te Kanawa and José Carreras at the Proms in the park in Hyde Park.

After her retirement from singing, Kiri set up the Kiri Te Kanawa Foundation to support singers of all genres from her native New Zealand.

Diana Ross
born on 26th March 1944 in Vauxhall, Detroit, Michigan, USA

It is fitting that Ross, the 'Queen of Motown', was born in the Motor City of Detroit. She began her musical journey in the 1960s with The Supremes, a trio that achieved immense success with hits like *Baby Love, Stop! In the Name of Love* and *You Can't Hurry Love*. The group's harmonies and Ross's distinctive voice made them trailblazers in the world of R&B and pop music. In 1970, Diana Ross embarked on a solo career that further solidified her status as a musical legend. Her solo career produced chart-toppers such as *Ain't No Mountain High Enough*, *Upside Down*, *I'm Coming Out* and *Endless Love*, a duet with Lionel Richie. Her powerful vocals, stage presence and glamorous image captivated audiences worldwide, including when she performed on the Pyramid stage at Glastonbury in 2022. Beyond her music, she made her mark in Hollywood, earning an Academy Award nomination for her role as Billie Holiday in the biographical film *Lady Sings the Blues*. Diana Ross remains an influential figure, with a career spanning decades. She has won numerous accolades, including Grammy Awards, a Kennedy Center Honor, and inductions into the Rock and Roll Hall of Fame and the Songwriters Hall of Fame.

Ross was awarded the Presidential Medal of Freedom, the nation's highest civilian award, by President Obama in a live televised ceremony held in the East Room of the White House on the 22nd November 2016.

Leonard Gordon Goodman
born on 24th April 1944 in Farnborough, Kent, UK

In April 2004, the BBC took a huge gamble. Desperate to find a new show with mass appeal, it had come up with a seemingly bizarre solution. Ballroom dancing was deeply unfashionable. The quickstep and jive hailed from a bygone age. Now, the corporation was attempting to make the nostalgic preserve of a few elderly enthusiasts the centrepiece of its Saturday nights. Just days before the first show, the producers hit a crisis. Four judges had been offered contracts: Craig Revel Horwood, Arlene Phillips, Bruno Tonioli and a well-known figure from the world of dance. At the very last moment, the fourth judge dropped out. The BBC was at a loss. Dozens of former world champions, giants of their profession, had already been interviewed, but none had been right. The show's professional dancers were asked if any luminaries had been missed. Erin Boag, a former New Zealand champion, tentatively offered a suggestion: "Have you tried Len Goodman?", she asked. "He's just a dance teacher from Dartford, but he's a bit of a character." The rest, as they say, is history. Goodman was not only a natural dancer and also the most knowledgeable of the panel on the subject of ballroom dancing, he also had great comedic timing.

For more than a decade, Goodman crossed the Atlantic twice a week appearing as head judge on both the UK and US versions of the show. While in Los Angeles, he shared an apartment complex with Tonioli, with Bruno doing the cooking and Len the ironing.

George Walton Lucas Jr.
born on 14th May 1944 in Modesto, California, USA

On graduating from the University of Southern California in 1967, Lucas co-founded American Zoetrope with his fellow filmmaker Francis Ford Coppola. Lucas wrote and directed *THX 1138* (1971), based on his student short film. It was a critical success, but a financial failure. His next job as a screenwriter-director was the movie *American Graffiti* (1973). It was inspired by his adolescence in the 1960s in Modesto, California, and produced through the newly created Lucasfilm. One big problem for Lucas was that on completion, there was no money left to pay all the crew. Lucas hit upon the idea of giving all the crew credits in lieu of immediate payment. They accepted and thus started the tradition of huge trailer credits at the end of movies. The money quickly rolled in as the movie was a critical and commercial success receiving five nominations for the Oscars, including Best Picture. His next project *Star Wars* (1977) would change both Lucas' life and cinema history forever. It is the second most watched film in movie history, behind *Gone With the Wind*. After the first Star Wars movie, Lucas produced and co-wrote the following instalments in the trilogy, *The Empire Strikes Back* (1980) and *The Return of the Jedi* (1983). Together with Steven Spielberg, Lucas co-created and helped collaborate with the stories of the *Indiana Jones* movie series. He also directed three further prequel films in the *Star Wars* series. In 2012, he sold Lucasfilm to the The Walt Disney Company for a reported $4 billion. Lucas refuses to put 'critics quotes' on his movie posters; something that infuriates many critic societies.

Sir Raymond Douglas Davies CBE
born on 21st June 1944 in London, UK

Ray Davies is the eldest of eight children born to Fred and Annie Davies. He was exposed to music from a young age, as his father was a jazz musician and his mother was a fan of classical music. In 1964, he formed the band The Kinks with his brother Dave. The band quickly gained popularity and released their debut album, *Kinks* in 1964 which featured the hit single *You Really Got Me*, which became a worldwide hit. The band went on to release several successful albums, including *Something Else by The Kinks* (1967), *The Kinks Are the Village Green Preservation Society* (1968), and *Lola Versus Powerman and the Moneygoround* (1970). In the 1970s, Ray Davies began to focus more on his solo career, releasing his debut solo album *The Village Green Preservation Society* in 1972. The album was a critical and commercial success featuring the hit single *Celluloid Heroes*. He followed this up with the albums *Preservation Act 1* (1973) and *Preservation Act 2* (1974). In the 1980s, he released several more solo albums, including *Give the People What They Want* (1981), *Word of Mouth* (1984) and *Think Visual* (1986). He also released the album *Return to Waterloo* (1985), which was a soundtrack to the film of the same name. In August 2015, Davies was voted the 27th greatest songwriter of all time by Rolling Stone Magazine. He was also knighted in the 2017 New Years Honours for services to the arts.

The song *Lola* was banned by the BBC for featuring the drink Coca Cola, which was against their policy banning product placement. Davies interrupted a tour in 1970 to race back to London to change the lyric to 'cherry cola'.

Geoffrey Arnold 'Jeff' Beck
born on 24th June 1944 in Wallington, Surrey, England

Jeff Beck's name runs through music, like that of a seaside town through a stick of rock. He was renowned as a pioneering guitarist who pushed the boundaries of the instrument to places unknown to most of his contemporaries. Beck could more than hold his own with fellow luminaries such as Jimmy Page and Eric Clapton (all three of them played in the Yardbirds). Yet unlike them, Beck was something of a reluctant celebrity unwilling to pursue the super-stardom that his musical gifts could have brought him. "When Led Zeppelin made it so big, I was jealous, absolutely jealous as hell", Beck said in 1986, "But I'm glad I carried on as I was. I personally couldn't have put up with that mass adulation." When Clapton and Page appeared at Live Aid in 1985, Beck preferred to stay at home and tinker with his beloved collection of classic hot rod cars. "I didn't want to go, because I hate large crowds," he claimed. Beck's gifts burned most intensely after he left the Yardbirds in November 1966 and formed the first incarnation of the Jeff Beck Group in early 1967. In 1975, Beck re-emerged in a jazz-inflected guise with the all-instrumental album *Blow by Blow*. It became Beck's most successful album, reaching No. 4 on the US chart and selling a million copies. Beck's last live show was on 12th November 2022 at the Grand Sierra Resort in Reno. He was joined on stage by good buddy Johnny Depp. Beck died in January 2023 aged 78.

When Stevie Wonder invited Beck to perform on his 1972 album *Talking Book*, the great guitarist agreed on condition that Wonder write a song for him. The result was *Superstition*.

Sir Clive Hubert Lloyd CBE AO
born on 31st August 1944 in Georgetown, British Guiana (Guyana)

Lloyd left school at age 14 to support his family, but spent his spare time playing cricket. After a stellar club career in his native Guyana, he was called up into the West Indies team in 1966 to play alongside the likes of Gary Sobers and Lance Gibbs. When Lloyd joined the team, there were two main problems. Talented though they were, the West Indies played 'Calypso Cricket', fun to watch, but with poor results. In addition, the team, who played in front of packed audiences, were paid a pittance. By the time Lloyd left the scene, both problems had been solved. A tall, hulking left-handed batsman who wore thick glasses and wielded an unusually heavy bat, Lloyd could drive and hook the ball with tremendous power. In a Test career spanning 110 matches, he averaged nearly 47 runs per innings, had 19 centuries and a top score of 242 runs. He was also a skilled medium-pace bowler and, early in his career, an excellent cover fielder. As captain he unleashed 'The Four Pacemen of The Apocalypse': Holding, Croft, Garner and Roberts, a fearsome foursome. He was also instrumental in persuading many of his teammates to join Kerry Packer's World Cricket breakaway series, where the cricketers were better rewarded. When the players returned to the fold they found that their pay had increased markedly. He was knighted in 2020.

Lloyd led the West Indies to two World Cup championships and a record 36 Test victories, including 11 consecutive wins. He was much loved in Lancashire, where he helped the county to three successive 'limited overs' cup victories.

Barry Eugene Carter aka Barry White
born on 12th September 1944 in Galveston, Texas, USA

White's early life was troubled, but he landed on his feet. At age 16, he was jailed for stealing a consignment of Cadillac tyres. While in jail, he listened to Elvis Presley's *It's Now or Never* on the radio which inspired him to sing. Dubbed 'The Maestro', White went on to a stunningly successful career as a pop singer that spanned five decades, and made him a star of the disco era. Having written several new songs and recorded his vocals for demo purposes only, White was surprised and reluctant when 20th Century Records pushed him to release the songs under his own name. When he finally did so in 1973, he quickly established himself as a star. From 1973 to 1977, sometimes under his own name and sometimes under the name *Love Unlimited Orchestra*, White recorded a string of steamy soul classics that featured his resonant bass voice speaking and singing over lush orchestral arrangements of subject matter clearly expressed in his song titles alone: *Can't Get Enough Of Your Love, Babe*, *Your Sweetness Is My Weakness*, *It's Ecstasy When You Lay Down Next To Me* and *I'm Gonna Love You Just A Little More, Baby*. White died in 2003 aged just 58. In an obituary referring to White by his nickname, 'The Walrus of Love', the BBC described him as having the rich timbres of one of the most distinctive soul voices of his generation, about which it was once said: "If chocolate fudge cake could sing, it would sound like Barry White."

In 1989 Lisa Stansfield wrote *All Around the World* as a tribute to Barry White. The pair would later record it as a duet.

 ### Winifred Jacqueline Fraser Bisset LdH
born on 13th September 1944 in Weybridge, Surrey, UK

Jacqueline Bisset is known for her captivating beauty, versatile acting skills and longevity in film and television. Her career began in the 1960s when she appeared in various British films before gaining international recognition in the 1970s. One of her most iconic roles came in 1973 when she starred opposite Steve McQueen in the classic film *The Getaway*. Her natural talent and on-screen presence garnered critical acclaim and a devoted fan following. Bisset's elegance and charisma have made her a timeless Hollywood star. Throughout her career, Bisset has received numerous awards and nominations, including a Golden Globe Award for her performance in the 2013 miniseries *Dancing on the Edge*. Her filmography boasts a wide range of genres, from neo-noir movies like *Bullitt* to action-packed thrillers like *The Deep*. She has also made notable appearances in French cinema. She starred in François Truffaut's *Day for Night* (1973), which won the Academy Award for Best Foreign Language Film. Her French filmography also includes *Le Magnifique* (1973) and *La Cérémonie* (1995). When she accepted a Golden Globe Award for her role in the British TV miniseries *Dancing on the Edge* in 2014, she reminded the audience that it had been 47 years since she had first been honoured by the Hollywood Foreign Press Association.

Bisset was one of the first actresses to earn a seven-figure fee for a single performance. She was paid $1.65 million to appear in *Inchon* (1981) alongside Lawrence Olivier. It flopped and for many years held the record as being the largest financial failure in cinema history.

 ### Michael Kirk Douglas
born on 25th September 1944 in New Brunswick, New Jersey, USA

Michael Douglas is the son of film legend Kirk Douglas and British actress Diana Dill. He is famous for his acting roles in films including *Romancing the Stone*, *Basic Instinct*, *Fatal Attraction* and *Wall Street*, for which he won an Oscar. What is less well known about him is that he has been one of the most influential figures behind the camera. Having got his big break playing opposite Karl Malden in TV's *The Streets of San Francisco* (1972), Douglas used his spare time to produce a screen rendering of *One Flew Over The Cuckoo's Nest* (1975), for which his father had secured the rights. From this triumph, Douglas went on to produce some of the biggest box-office hits of the next two decades, including *Starman* (1984), *Flatliners* (1990), *Face/Off* (1997) and *The Rainmaker* (1997). In 2018, Douglas combined acting and producing in television's *The Kominsky Method*, in which he played an actor who years ago had a dalliance with success and is now a revered Hollywood acting coach. The highly acclaimed series must have felt like an old school reunion for Douglas as he appeared alongside Kathleen Turner, Nancy Travis and Alan Arkin in his last role. The dialogue between Douglas and Arkin, which usually takes place over drinks or a meal is both funny and semi-autobiographical.

Douglas has the dubious distinction of winning the Most Egregious Age Difference Between the Leading Man and the Love Interest Award given by the Alliance of Women Film Journalists. They were for *Solitary Man* and *Last Vegas*.

 ## Bernard Hill
born on 17th December 1944 in Blackley, Manchester, UK

Bernard Hill is one of Britain's finest character actors. Born in Manchester, his acting career began in amateur theatre with the Salford Players. He made his English television debut in 1973 in Mike Leigh's first film, *Hard Labour*. However, it was his searing portrayal of Yosser Hughes, the desperate, out-of-work head-butting Scouser in Alan Bleasdale's *The Boys From the Blackstuff* (1980), that announced his arrival as an actor of note. Hill's powerful depiction of a man crumbling before your eyes brought him a mantlepiece full of awards but, as he later revealed, almost "drove him to the edge of insanity". Yosser came to represent the desperation of Britain's unemployed and his catchphrase "Gizza job" entered the nation's consciousness. He has appeared in Sir Richard Attenborough's Oscar-winning *Gandhi* (1982) and played Pauline Collins' husband in *Shirley Valentine* (1989). Other film credits include some of the most successful films of all time. Among them *Titanic* (1997), where he played the unfortunate Captain Smith and *Lord of The Rings: The Return of the King* (2003). On stage, Hill has played leading roles in Arthur Miller's *A View from the Bridge*, Chekov's *The Cherry Orchard* and the most demanding Shakespearean role of all, *Macbeth*.

Hill has the distinction of being the only actor to have appeared in more than one film that won 11 Academy Awards: *Lord of the Rings: The Return of the King* and *Titanic*. He did not appear in *Ben Hur*, the only other film to date that has won 11 Oscars.

Other Notable Births

 Jimmy Page
9th January 1944
Musician

Smokin' Joe Frazier
12th January 1944
Boxer

 Bobby Ball
28th January 1944
Comedian | Actor

 Roger Lloyd-Pack
8th February 1944
Actor

 Alan Parker
14th February 1944
Film Director

 Sir Ranulph Fiennes
7th March 1944
Explorer | Writer

 Pattie Boyd
17th March 1944
Model | Photographer

 Joe Cocker
20th May 1944
Singer

 Gladys Knight
28th May 1944
Singer | Songwriter

 Ernő Rubik
13th July 1944
Inventor

 John Simpson
9th August 1944
Journalist

 Angela Rippon
12th October 1944
Journalist | Presenter

 Tim Rice
10th November 1944
Lyricist | Author

 Danny DeVito
17th November 1944
Actor | Comedian

 Brenda Lee
11th December 1944
Singer

Sir Edwin Landseer Lutyens
died aged 74 on 1st January 1944 in Marylebone, London, UK

After graduating from the Royal College of Art, Lutyens was articled in 1877 to a firm of architects but soon branched out on his own. His early work was influenced by his Surrey surroundings and was traditional. His style changed when he met landscape gardener Gertrude Jekyll, who taught him 'simplicity of intention and directness of purpose.' At Munstead Wood, Godalming, Surrey (1896), Lutyens first showed his personal qualities as a designer. A series of similar buildings followed. In 1912, he was selected to advise on the planning of the new Indian capital at Delhi. New Delhi, as it became known, was a garden city on a grand scale, based on a series of hexagons separated by tree lined avenues. After the Great War, Lutyens became architect to the Imperial War Graves Commission, for which he designed the Cenotaph and the Great War Stone, a memorial placed at sites of over 1,000 war dead. His last, vast project was the Roman Catholic Cathedral in Liverpool which was incomplete at his death.

Ida Minerva Tarbell
died aged 86 on 6th January 1944 in Bridgeport, Connecticut, USA

Ida was a pioneer of modern investigative journalism. She was the only woman in her graduating class at Allegheny College in 1880. She was first employed at *McClure's* magazine where she exposed the unfair practices of the Standard Oil Company; this lead to a US Supreme Court decision to break its monopoly. Returning to her home city of Pennsylvania, Tarbell became acquainted with the editor of a small magazine called *The Chautauquan* and was offered a job with the journal. She worked there for nearly a decade, holding various positions before becoming its managing editor. In 1890, however, she left both the paper and the country, moving overseas to Paris for several years to pursue graduate studies at the Sorbonne and the College de France. She left *McClure's* in 1906 and for the next nine years wrote for *American Magazine*, of which she was also a co-owner and co-editor. She also wrote eight biographies of Abraham Lincoln.

Edvard Munch
died aged 80 on 23rd April 1944 in Oslo, Norway

Born near Oslo into a middle-class family, Munch was a painter and print maker whose intensely evocative treatment of psychological themes were built on the main tenets of late 19th century symbolism which greatly influenced early 20th century German Expressionism. His 1893 painting *The Scream* (alternatively titled *The Cry*), can be seen as a symbol of modern existential anguish. Between 1893 and 1910, he made two painted versions and two in pastels, as well as a number of prints. One of the pastels would eventually sell for $119.9 million at Sotherby's in May 2012. Munch's family had profoundly influenced his art. His mother died when he was five, his eldest sister when he was 14, both having contracted tuberculosis. He would capture the latter event in his masterpiece, *The Sick Child*. Munch's father and brother also died when he was young and another sister suffered from acute mental illness. "Illness, insanity and death", as he said "were the black angels that kept watch over my cradle and accompanied me all my life."

Joseph Patrick Kennedy Jr.

died aged 29 on 12th August 1944 over Blythburgh, East Suffolk, UK

World War II produced many "what if?" moments, but probably none bigger than "what if a different Kennedy brother died?" In 1943, John F. Kennedy, the man who would go on to be 35th President of The United States, swam miles to safety after his boat was torpedoed by the Japanese Navy. In 1944, his elder brother Joseph, was not so fortunate. In a family where expectations ran high, Joseph Jr.'s grandfather John Fitzgerald, who had been mayor of Boston, stated that his grandson would grow up to be the first Catholic President of the United States. In the summer of 1944, Joe Jr. volunteered for a secret bombing campaign. His mission, along with co-pilot Wilford John Willy, was to fly over Normandy, France in a radio-controlled B-17 bomber to a German V-2 rocket launching site, arm the explosives stowed on board, and then parachute to safety before detonation. On the evening of 12th August, the explosives on the plane detonated prematurely. Their bodies were never found.

Johannes Erwin Eugen Rommel

died aged 52 on 14th October 1944 in Herrlingen, Nazi Germany

Few of the major players of WWII have been the subject of more debate than Rommel. For many he was seen as the 'Good Nazi', but he was never a member of the Nazi Party. He was, however, an enthusiastic supporter of Hitler's expansionist policies and must have known of the atrocities committed by the regime. When German tanks rolled into Poland in 1939, he was tasked with guarding Hitler. He then pushed for his own Panza Division. In 1940, he spearheaded the German invasions of Belgium, The Netherlands and France. He then commanded the Afrika Korps and had great success until the Allies promoted Montgomery when he met his match. As the Nazis retreated back into Europe, he commanded a depleted defence force, in an unsuccessful attempt to thwart the Allied invasion. Finally, when he was implicated in a plot to assassinate Hitler, he was forced to take his own life. The German public were told that he had died in battle and he was afforded a State Funeral.

Alton Glen (Glenn) Miller

died aged 41 on 15th December 1944 over the English Channel

On a mid-December day, a single-engined Noorduyn Norseman aircraft left Twinwood Farm airbase in south-east England for Paris, carrying the hottest big-band leader of the era, Glenn Miller. Within two minutes, the plane had vanished into the fog and not a trace was ever found, nor any reason for its disappearance established. Glenn Miller was the man who put American bobbysoxers *In The Mood* for jiving and sent them swooning to their beds with a *Moonlight Serenade*. With his bland features, thin lips and Wall Street rimless glasses, Miller looked as straight as you can get, but he was one of the biggest pop stars of his day. His reputation was only enhanced when he patriotically disbanded his band in 1942 at the height of its popularity to lead the Glenn Miller Army Air Force Band. He was setting out for Paris to organise a Christmas concert for the troops in liberated Paris when he disappeared. Miller's name is engraved on the 'Tablets of the Missing' at the Cambridge (UK) American Cemetery and Memorial.

The Coins We Used

27 years before decimalisation, we used the system of pounds, shillings and pence commonly represented using the symbols **£sd**. The **£** symbol evolved over many years from the letter L which derives from the Latin word libra, meaning a pound of money. Although **s** is the first letter of the word shilling, the use of the letter derives from the Latin word solidus which means coin. The curious use of the letter **d** for pennies also has a Latin origin from the word denarius meaning containing ten. Unlike the decimal system based on multiples of 10, the pre-decimal system was based on multiples of 12. There were 12 pennies to a shilling and 240 pennies to a pound. This meant there were 20 shillings to the pound. In 1944, there were 9 coins in circulation with evocative names that still permeate our language today.

Farthing ¼ d
In use to 1961

With 4 farthings to a penny, these smallest of coins featured a smooth edge and a wren on the reverse. *He hasn't got two farthings to rub together* was a popular expression to describe someone poor.

Halfpenny ½ d
In use to 1969

Commonly known as the ha'penny it is was the only word in the English language with a silent 'f'. Since 1937, the coin featured Sir Francis Drake's ship The Golden Hind. The popular pub game Shove Ha'penny features 5 halfpennies.

Penny 1d
In use to 1971

Pre 1860, the penny was a large copper coin. This is why bicycles with a large front wheel were nicknamed Penny Farthings. Popular expressions using the penny include *ten a penny* and *penny for your thoughts*.

Threepence 3d
In use to 1971

These 12-sided coins were commonly known as *thruppence* or *thrupenny bits*. The silver versions known as joeys were often hidden in Christmas puddings, making an exciting find for the lucky children who discovered them.

Sixpence 6d
In use to 1980

These silver coins reputedly brought good luck. Sixpences were placed in bride's shoes as a wedding gesture. Known as benders, they could easily be bent. *Going on a bender* derived from drinking all day in pubs with sixpence.

Shilling 1/-
In use to 1990

First minted in the reign of Henry VII as a testoon, the shilling was latterly commonly known as a bob. *Taking the king's shilling* meant enrolling in the army whilst *A few bob short of a pound* describes someone a bit mad.

Florin 2/-
In use to 1992

The florin was Britain's first decimal coin in response to calls in the mid 19th century for decimal coinage to be introduced. As 2 *bob*, the florin was worth 1/10th of a pound. After decimalisation in 1971 florins became worth 10 pence.

Half Crown 2/6
In use to 1969

Half crowns were originally struck in gold in the reign of Henry VIII. The first silver half crowns were issued under Edward VII in 1557. Surviving for over 450 years, the Half Crown was one of the most successful coins of all time.

Crown 5/-
In use to present day

The British crown is a heavy silver coin. Rarely spent, crowns are often minted for commemorative purposes. After decimalisation, a crown was worth 25p until 1990 when their face value was changed to £5.

The average annual salary in the UK in 1944 was approximately:

£210 - £290

Although commercial car production effectively ceased during the war, prices remained virtually static pre and post war. This example of a Morris 8 Series E, launched in 1938, would cost:

£175

The price of the average house would be approximately 3-4x the average annual salary. Depending on where you were in the country this meant the price of a typical 1930's 3-bedroom semi-detached house would be in the region of:

£720 - £960

The above Utility Radio or Wartime Civilian Receiver was a standardised radio developed by British radio manufacturers during the war. It cost:

£12 3s 4d

The maximum retail price of bread per lb (including National Wheatmeal Bread) was:

2d

A dozen Grade II eggs would cost a maximum of:

2s 3d

Working Life in the Factory

In 1944 the factory largely meant one place, the munitions factory. Virtually all industrial production had been turned over to producing instruments of war. As large numbers of our men had gone abroad to do their bit, it was once more the role of women to stand in and undertake work that would usually be the domain of men. Women were recruited with posters reminding them that the lives of their husbands, lovers and brothers depended on their work. During the war over one million women worked in munitions factories and while the financial rewards were relatively high, so were the risks. The factories operated using production lines and often very little training was given. The women were quickly shown what to do and then did it. Shells had to be loaded with hot TNT dispensed by a machine akin to a cement mixer. Then, a detonator had to be attached. The work was arduous, boring and repetitive and required great powers of concentration as the filling of every shell was fraught with risk. Another big danger came from the fact that a direct hit from an enemy bomb might obliterate the whole factory killing those inside. For fear that morale would be damaged, most accidents and fatalities were not widely reported. One incident that could not be kept hushed up was the explosion of Naval bombs on 30th May 1944 at the Rotherwas factory in Hereford. Dozens of firefighters fought for hours to stop millions of pounds worth of explosives from igniting which would have destroyed the whole city. Miraculously, only two people lost their lives. Aside from the risks of explosion, the materials the workers handled were extremely toxic with any contact with the face requiring immediate medical attention. Apart from the physical danger, the chemicals turned many women's hair orange and their skin yellow. Hours were long and the factories were open around the clock; sometimes the women were required to work eighty-plus hour weeks. The pay, however, was good though not anywhere equal to a man's salary. It was the first time in British history that ordinary women had so much disposable income. Their wages were spent on almost any luxury item they could get their hands on be it cosmetics, stockings or handbags. Black marketeers had a field day. The women were cash rich and time poor. When given time off, they partied hard like there was no tomorrow, in the knowledge that for many there might not be one. Britain could not have emerged victorious without the help of these women who worked all hours to supply our armed forces. After a long running campaign, in 2012, 18 of the munitions workers finally got to lay a wreath at the cenotaph on Remembrance Day to honour their fallen comrades.

Working in a munitions factory

GECO Munitions factory, Scarborough

Clocking off at the end of a long day

Working Life on the Farm

Farming in the UK during the Second World War underwent a complete upheaval. It was essential that the government controlled what farmers grew and what livestock they kept, in order to maximise nutritional output. For example, the government sought to place limits on the production of meat as this was considered wasteful. It encouraged growing of vegetables rich in carbohydrates such as potatoes. Food that had been imported from the Empire before the war was no longer available, and American food aid had only just begun to arrive. The Ministry of Agriculture also instigated a programme of culling animals classed as pests. Deer, rabbits, birds and rats were killed in large numbers. Most would end up as part of a hearty stew, but hopefully not the rats. 1944 was a good year to be a farmer, there was increased mechanisation and food inflation was rife, the Government also handed out generous subsidies. Day-to-day life on the farm also changed markedly from before the war. Many men had joined the armed forces and there was a shortage of labour. At first, many women signed up to join the Women's Land Army (WLA) and they helped to increase food production greatly. However, by 1942, the attraction of farm work had faded. Women were paid only half the rate of men doing the same often backbreaking job, living conditions were often appalling and the cities from which most of the women came were now safer as Germany's ability to bomb them had been undermined. The year saw what had been a voluntary service being replaced by conscription. By 1944, a peak of 80,000 'land girls' were working across the UK. Lady Gertrude Denman, Director of the WLA, once said "The land army fights in

Women's Land Army harvesting beets

Naval ratings lifting their parsnip crop

Weaning a calf on a farm in Dartington

the fields. It is in the fields of Britain that the most critical battle of the present war may well be fought and won." Women undertook all aspects of farm work, including livestock handling, dairy, flax growing (for clothing), hedging, vegetable growing, ploughing, threshing and lumber-jilling (the female equivalent of lumber-jacking). The unemployed from the cities, conscientious objectors and prisoners of war were also put to work on the farm. The male farm workers who remained at home, especially the skilled ones, saw their pay increase markedly, this was done with the full backing of the Government as they were considered essential to the war effort. Membership of the National Union of Farmworkers trebled during the war, giving the workers even greater bargaining power.

Office Life

In 1944, office life was arcane both in the equipment used and in the social structures it imposed. Men held nearly all of the managerial posts and women's roles were mainly secretarial. It was even the case that those, both men and women, who worked in the civil service had to ask permission of their boss if they wanted to marry. Some who were refused had no option but to leave the service if they wanted to continue with their nuptials. The two main means of communication were the telephone and typed letters, often transcribed from shorthand notes. Although the photocopier had been invented before the war, it was in the early stage of development and had not made its way from America. Copies had to be made using carbon paper fitted between plain sheets. There was a limit to how many could be produced and the secretaries had to bang hard on the keys of the manual typewriter to make them legible, slowing down their work and creating an almighty din in the office. Computers did exist but these were used mainly to decipher enemy codes, no-one had yet foreseen their use in the office. One group of office workers who had the most demanding though probably the most rewarding job were those assigned to Prime Minister Winston Churchill. Churchill as well as being a great war leader was also an idiosyncratic character. There are stories of him giving dictation from the bath. The one male secretary was allowed in the room, but if he was unavailable the women would have to pin their ears to the door as he barked out his messages. He would also like to keep his staff on their toes saying things like "get me Ian from Sussex on the phone", knowing full well that the first time the secretary heard the order they would have no idea what he was talking about. In reality the word secretary hardly describes their roles. They were chauffeurs, international conference organisers, pet-sitters, purchasers of cigars and champagne and even worms for his fish. The modern day term for the roles would be personal assistant or office manager but these were different times. Despite the travails of working in the War Office, all his staff spoke fondly of working there and in those most demanding of times enjoyed being part of Churchill's team. Elizabeth Nel, his secretary who accompanied him to the Yalta Conference, said of the PM: "That great man - who could at any time be impatient, kind, irritable, crushing, generous, inspiring, difficult, alarming, amusing, unpredictable, considerate, seemingly impossible to please, charming, demanding, inconsiderate, quick to anger and quick to forgive - was unforgettable. One loved him with a deep devotion. Difficult to work for - yes, mostly; lovable - always; amusing - without fail."

19-year-old typist Iris Joyce

The Telephone Service HQ

Churchill at 10 Downing Street

Training for War in 1944

Many young men who had been barely in their teens at the outbreak of World War II in 1939, had now reached the age of 18 so call-up papers started landing on their doormats. In order to carry out a successful invasion of Europe, many more young men had to be trained in the art of fighting. The young men were ordered to go to assembly points, where they were herded into military vehicles and taken to training camps. For many this was a frightening experience as they had never left the comfort of home before. The camps consisted of a series of huts and new recruits were greeted by scenes of soldiers with rifles throwing themselves to the ground, shooting live ammunition. All too soon

Rifle drill at the start a gruelling day's training

that would be the lot of the freshmen. Accommodation in the huts was rudimentary to say the least. Each recruit was allocated a berth in a bunk bed, but very often there was jostling for the best position. After that the newbies had to fall in outside and were given a knife, fork and spoon each. Then there was the food. If they thought the meals they had at home were basic, they were in for a surprise. The order of the day was usually reconstituted potatoes, beans and a stringy substance purporting to be meat. After dinner the recruits had to wash their plates and cutlery in a vat of boiling water and report to their quarters. For many, the first night was the worst. The bed was hard and the pillow stuffed with straw. Reveille was at 6am and the recruits were ushered in to the wash room to shave and clean themselves. Then there was a visit to the stores where each man was issued with two battle dress uniforms, an overcoat, a rifle and a bayonet and all the accoutrements for soldiering. The reality of the situation came home when the regimental barber shaved each man's head to stubble. Many held back a tear for fear of looking weak; they were well and truly in the army now. The training, by necessity, was intense. From dawn until dusk the men were kept busy. The day started with rifle drill. Then it was on to physical training: an assault course and a five mile run. By the weekend the recruit was given a break, but only to have inoculations. Each man stood in a queue with a bared arm into which was plunged a large blunt needle. Some men fainted. By Monday morning the men, with arms numbed by the injections, had to start their training over again: marching, rifle drill and assault course training. This harsh regime was obviously designed to turn callow youth into soldiers, ready for war, irrespective of the price, which in some instances caused some of the recruits to attempt suicide. Many of these soldiers, who were barely men, found themselves fighting to liberate Europe from Nazi oppression, We are grateful to them for their sacrifice.

Physical training on the assault course

Relaxing in the living room of their suburban London home, the Chillingworth family gather around the fire. Whilst Sydney reads the newspaper, his wife Hilda is darning a sock. Their daughter, Jill, is knitting a scarf whilst her brother, Jeremy, is playing with his toy castle.

Mrs. Day is carefully sorting the cinders from the ash from last night's fire. She will re-use the cinders in the grate for today's fire, whilst the ash will be saved to help fertilise the garden.

In Eltham, South-East London, Mr. and Mrs. Suter are enjoying some fresh bread and a pot of tea at breakfast time in their family home.

Back in the Chillingworth house, it is 8 o'clock in the morning and Mrs. Chillingworth is helping her two children get ready for school. Sydney, her husband, has been working on night duty at the local fire station, as he works for the National Fire Service.

As it gets dark, seven-year-old Doreen Buckner draws the curtains at home in London. To ensure no light escapes into the night sky, every house also has blackout curtains across every window.

With so many essential supplies rationed, The Ministry of Food encouraged people to cook their entire meal in the oven to minimise how much fuel they used.

Furniture

'Make do and mend' were the watchwords of life during the austerity of the Second World War. Due to enemy disruption of British supplies from its Empire, everyday materials that were once in abundant supply, were now scarce. For most buying from new was no longer an option. The only new furniture produced during the war came under a strict government rationing scheme. In 1941, the Board of Trade designed a collection of furniture that could be produced cheaply and was of simple design. In 1942, Sir Hugh Dalton, President of the Board of Trade announced their aim was: "To secure the production of furniture of sound construction, in simple but agreeable designs and at reasonable prices." The furniture went on general sale in 1943. The original catalogue contained 30 pieces, their design being overseen by leading furniture designer Gordon Russell. Every piece had to comply with Utility Scheme standards and was stamped CC41 (Controlled Commodity 1941).

Only newly-weds or those whose homes had suffered significant bomb damage could apply for a permit to buy the furniture. A points system was put in place, each household would receive up to 30 points. Two chairs were worth 12 points and a sideboard 8, leaving little room for anything else. Very soon after the arrival of this furniture, a small and illegal cottage industry grew up where people would adorn the plain furniture and attempt to sell it at higher prices. After the war, utility furniture slowly fell out of favour as people became able to afford a more decorative style. It has however gone through periodic revivals. Today, furniture which bears the mark CC41 does well at auction.

Woolton Pie

Woolton pie, named after Frederick Marquis 1st Lord Woolton, was a pastry dish of vegetables suggested to the British people when shortages, particularly of meat, made other dishes hard to prepare. Though it was created by the head chef at the Savoy Hotel in London, it was rather an austere product and soon fell out of favour after the war.

Recipe

The ingredients can be varied according to which vegetables are in season.

For the filling

1lb carrots
1lb swede
1lb potatoes
1lb cauliflower
1 heaped teaspoon vegetable extract
1 heaped tablespoon oatmeal
A handful of parsley

For the pastry

3oz of fat, lard, margarine or butter
5oz wheatmeal or plain flour
1 teaspoon baking powder
4oz cooled, cooked potatoes
Salt to taste

Method: Place all the filling ingredients, save the parsley, into a pan with just enough water to cover. Cook on a medium to high heat and stir frequently to stop the mixture sticking. After 10 minutes the vegetables should yield to a knife still yet be intact. Place in a pie dish, sprinkle with parsley and allow to cool in the dish. For the pastry: beat the fat with a fork until soft and then work in the flour, potato, baking powder and salt through a sieve. Work the mixture by hand into a pliable dough and then roll out. Cover the vegetable mixture with the pastry and place in a moderate oven until the pastry is nicely golden. Serve with brown gravy.

Carrot Cake

One recipe that did not only survive the war, but thrived, was carrot cake. Strict sugar rationing meant that other sources of sweetness had to be found. Whilst many root vegetables such as swedes and parsnips were used, the carrot was favoured for its texture and colour. One big difference between the cake of 1944 and that of today is that you would have been extremely lucky to find it topped with icing.

Recipe

Ingredients

6oz plain flour
1 level teaspoon baking powder
3oz fat, lard, margarine or butter (or a mixture of each)
3oz oatmeal
1½ tablespoons sugar
1 grated medium sized carrot (2 if sugar is unavailable)
1 powdered egg (reconstituted) or 1 fresh egg
1 dessert spoon syrup
Water to mix

Method: Rub the fat into the flour, add the dry ingredients and the carrots and mix, stirring thoroughly. Add the egg and syrup and stir, add sufficient water to form a fairly stiff mixture. Transfer to a greased tin and bake in a moderate oven. After about 40 minutes test the cake with a knife, if it comes out clean the cake is cooked. Allow to cool on a baking rack and then serve. Store in a tin and eat within one week.

Holidays

Before the war, foreign holidays for the people of Britain were the domain of the wealthy. From 1939 this was no longer an option, even for those who could afford them. In other parts of the world, like North America, holidays were possible although more difficult as resources such as petrol and trains were being diverted to the war effort. By 1944, the British Government's 'Holidays at Home' scheme was in full swing. Its aim was to dissuade people from making long trips by highlighting previously neglected attractions of people's home towns. Take-up by local authorities was patchy. Edinburgh council was one organisation that backed the scheme wholeheartedly. Picnics, games, music, singing, dancing and raffles were organised, all against the magnificent backdrop of Arthur's Seat. Though no match for a real holiday, people could make believe and look forward to a time when actual holidays would be possible.

Arthur's Seat overlooking Edinburgh

Blackpool

Blackpool stood out as a place where people could holiday with some semblance of normality. In fact, the town thrived during the war. It had much going for it, accommodation was in plentiful supply as were the people to fill it. Many civil servants had relocated from London, the town saw tens of thousands of airman billeted there and American service personnel were stationed at nearby Warton. Women from nearby factories and those who worked the land also descended on Blackpool to enjoy any precious leave they were granted. Blackpool also had the advantage of being almost totally safe from enemy bombing. During the war there was only one attack resulting in fatalities. The town was of little strategic importance and the Luftwaffe were reluctant to damage the iconic Blackpool Tower as it provided a good navigational aid. Plays that would have normally been performed in London's West End moved north to Blackpool. Many of the plays had a war theme including Terence Rattigan's love triangle *Flare Path* which played in 1944. All in all, if you had a choice of anywhere to take a break in Britain it would have been Blackpool, Lancashire's party town. The Americans brought with them money and luxuries boosting the local economy, while the arrival of thespians from London brought an air of culture. In 1944, the whole town had a holiday camp feel allowing people to let their hair down and recharge the batteries for the often daunting tasks that lay ahead.

Blackpool Tower

Crime

During the war as most of the population pulled together to defeat the enemy, a small but not inconsiderable section of the population seemed to be pulling in the opposite direction. From the commencement of the war in 1939 until its conclusion six years later, crime rose across the board in the UK by 57%. Bomb damaged London provided rich pickings for those willing to stoop so low, and there were even cases of emergency service workers helping themselves. On 13th April 1944, Sidney James Delasalle became another client of lead executioner Albert Pierrepoint, when he was hanged at Durham Prison for the murder of Ronald Murphy at North Country Army Camp after a row about rations. Gangland crime was rife in London as traditional cockney mobsters fought battles with Maltese, Jewish and Italian gangs. The presence of so many soldiers from home and abroad had led to a lucrative vice trade where the gangs were willing to use extreme violence to gain control over it. Rationing led to a flourishing black market where the gangs were ever present to exploit every opportunity. The fact that the capital saw many police officers join the army did not help. There were several jewellery heists carried out by a gang led by North London villain Billy Hill. Forgery and theft of ration books and clothing coupons were rife up and down the country; criminals found a ready market with people desperate to supplement their meagre rations. The Government books and coupons were so rudimentary that they were very easy to forge with few people were ever being prosecuted for producing or handling them. Conmen also took advantage. For example, a contractor conspired with a Hammersmith clerk of works to pass air-raid shelters as safe when they were anything but. Many people died as a result of this shoddy workmanship; manslaughter charges followed. When the Government planned the evacuation of children

A police sergeant in Wotton-under-Edge

A police motorcyclist calls the station

from our cities at the beginning of the war they hadn't bargained for the fact that nearly half would remain. By 1944, few schools were open and many children lived feral lives leading to a large increase in anti-social behaviour. Some of the increase in crime can, however, be put down to the fact that defence regulations brought in during the war meant that there were now more laws to break. Some seemingly minor infringements were punished harshly. Prosecutions for breaching regulations were no respecter of status. Ivor Novello, composer of the famous first world war song, *Keep the Home Fires Burning*, was sentenced to eight weeks (reduced to four) in 1944 for the fairly minor offence of the misuse of petrol coupons offered to him by a female fan. Noël Coward may have hit the nail on the head as to why the authorities came down so harshly on Novello when he observed "He's been fighting like a steer to keep going as before the war and hasn't done a thing for the general effort."

As can be seen from these photographs, despite raw materials being in short supply, wartime 'austerity' fashions were not drab. Here is a purple, green and mauve dress designed by well-known fashion designer Norman Hartnell. The dress cost 7 clothing coupons.

This scarlet wool Utility frock was designed by the fashion label Dorville and sold by John Lewis and Co. Ltd. It cost 11 coupons and 60/-.

This mustard-coloured wool Spectator dress cost 11 coupons. It is paired with a dark-coloured turban, a popular head wear item. The ensemble is finished with a handbag with large metal clasp.

In this rooftop setting, the model on the left is wearing a blue-flecked tweed Utility suit from fashion label Derata. The model on the right is wearing an emerald green woollen frock with matching jacket designed by Norman Hartnell. It cost 22 coupons.

This two-tone Atrima dress cost 7 coupons. In 1944, the clothes ration book had a total of 66 coupons in it.

Monsieur Jean, a master tailor at the house of designer Norman Hartnell, is pictured in the tailoring room cutting a model suit.

Here we see a scarlet and white spot-printed Utility rayon shirt dress with front-buttoning with accompanying white turban and white gloves. It was part of the Utility Clothing Scheme.

Here we see famous fashion designer Peter Russell sketching a new design in his London couture house.

Top 10 Girls' Baby Names [1]

1. **Margaret** — from *Margārīta*, the old Persian word meaning 'Pearl'
2. **Patricia** — of Latin origin meaning 'Noble Patrician'
3. **Christine** — of French and Latin origin meaning 'Follower of Christ'
4. **Mary** — from the Latin *Stella Maris* meaning 'Star of the Sea'
5. **Jean** — of Hebrew origin meaning 'God is gracious'
6. **Ann** — of Hebrew origin meaning 'God has favoured me'
7. **Susan** — of Hebrew origin meaning 'Lily Rose'
8. **Janet** — of French origin meaning little Joan itself meaning 'God's Gift'
9. **Maureen** — of Irish Gaelic origin meaning 'Star of the Sea'
10. **Barbara** — of Latin origin meaning 'Foreign Woman'

Top 10 Boys' Baby Names [2]

1. **John** — of Hebrew origin meaning 'God has been gracious'
2. **David** — of Hebrew origin meaning 'Beloved'
3. **Michael** — of Hebrew origin meaning 'Who is like God?'
4. **Peter** — from the Greek *Petros* meaning 'Rock'
5. **Robert** — from Old German meaning 'Bright Fame'
6. **Anthony** — of Latin origin meaning 'Priceless One'
7. **Brian** — of Celtic origin meaning 'Strong, High and Noble'
8. **Alan** — from Old German meaning 'Precious' or Gaelic meaning 'Little Rock'
9. **William** — of Old German origin meaning 'Resolute Protector'
10. **James** — from the Hebrew name *Jacob* meaning 'Supplanter'

[1] [2] Data compiled by the Office for National Statistics 1944

Games, Toys and Pastimes

Games, toys and pastimes have always reflected the attitude and imagination of the culture that created them. During the War children played many different games that were handed down to them and invented a few of their own. Group games such as hopscotch, statues and hide and seek were popular as they required little or no equipment. Ball games were often played with improvised equipment, for example a ball of rags for a football or a stick for a cricket bat. When real sports paraphernalia was available, children were at the mercy of their owner who could call an end to the game at any time. Board games such as chess and checkers were played as were newer family games like Scrabble and Monopoly. Adults played bridge and gin rummy whilst young children contented themselves with snap and happy families. Meccano, a model construction system consisting of metal strips and nuts and bolts was popular with both children and adults. Whilst no new sets were produced, old ones were dusted off and hours of fun were had.

Building with Meccano

Celebrating Christmas in 1944

During World War II, Christmas in Britain was a subdued affair. Many families had loved ones fighting overseas. The country was still experiencing the hardships of war, including rationing and bombing. However, the British people were resilient, and Christmas was still a time for celebration, even if it was a more modest one. Many people put up Christmas trees, although these were often small and not as elaborately decorated as they might be in peacetime. Present giving was also more difficult during the war due to rationing. Many people made their own gifts, such as knitwear or baked goods, or exchanged small items that they had been able to obtain. Others sent gifts to loved ones serving overseas. Christmas dinners were also more modest than they might have been in peacetime. The government had introduced rationing in 1940, which meant that people had to make do with less food. This included meat, which was in short supply. As a result, many Christmas dinners consisted of vegetables including potatoes, carrots and Brussels sprouts. Despite the difficulties, the British people still found ways to enjoy the holiday season. There were carol singing events, pantomimes and other festive gatherings. The BBC broadcast special Christmas programmes, which many people listened to on the radio. In 1944, King George VI gave a radio address on Christmas Day. The King spoke of hope in his message saying that "the lamps which the Germans had put out all over Europe were being rekindled and were beginning to shine through the fog of war." He added that "at this

Father Christmas handing out toys to evacuees

Christmas time we think proudly and gratefully of our fighting men wherever they may be."Overall, Christmas in Britain during 1944 was a time of both celebration and reflection. While the war was still ongoing, the people found ways to come together and enjoy the holiday season, despite the challenges they were facing. One popular holiday activity during this time was sending Christmas cards. Despite the difficulties of the war, people still found ways to communicate with each other and spread holiday cheer. Some created their own cards, using whatever materials they had to hand. Others

Christmas on-board HMS Malaya

purchased cards from shops, although these were often more expensive and harder to come by due to the war. In addition to Christmas cards, many people also exchanged letters and packages with loved ones serving overseas. These often contained small gifts, such as food or other necessities, as well as letters and photos. These exchanges were a way for people to stay connected with their loved ones and let them know they were thinking of them during the holiday season. While the war had a significant impact on Christmas in Britain in 1944, it did not diminish the spirit of the holiday. The British people were known for their resilience and determination, and they found ways to come together and celebrate despite the challenges they were facing. Even though V1 and V2 rockets were landing on the cities of Britain, Christmas 1944 was a time of hope as the D-Day Landings of June meant that the war should soon be over.

In 1944, entertainment provided civilians with a form of escape from the privations of life in wartime. It was also important to those serving in the forces at home and overseas. There was no television as it was feared that the strong signal from London's Alexandra Palace could serve as a navigational aide for enemy aircraft. So in September 1939 following a cartoon, *Mickey's Gala Premier*, television services were halted. TV service resumed on the 7th June 1946 and after a brief opening ceremony the BBC once again played the Mickey Mouse cartoon. By the start of the war, only 20,000 households had TV sets as compared to 10 million radio licences. The cinema was also hugely popular, with films such as Oscar-winning *Casablanca*, the tense psychological drama *Gaslight* and the hilarious *Arsenic and Old Lace* playing to packed houses. The films were often preceded by Pathé News, which gave audiences a heavily censored account of how the

Yehudi Menuhin

war was going. Theatres that had closed at the beginning of the war began to reopen. In September 1944, a lucky few witnessed Yehudi Menuhin give the first British performance of Béla Bartók's *Second Violin Concerto* in Bedford in an opening concert of a tour with the BBC Orchestra conducted by Adrian Boult. Not only were there no music charts in Britain in 1944, there was also no vinyl to make records. Production of polyvinyl chloride was used exclusively for the war effort. Instead people had to make do with music from the radio or pull out a record from their pre-war collection. Performers such as Flanagan and Allen and Vera Lynn were popular, as were Americans Bing Crosby and Judy Garland. British musical tastes were also widened by the influx of G.I.s who brought with them new musical genres such as Bebop, a fast-tempo form of jazz. The pub, that traditional hub of British life, provided homemade entertainment. Many a

Bing Crosby

round was interrupted by a sing-a-long of *Knees Up Mother Brown* or *Maybe its because I'm a Londoner*, which was composed by Hubert Gregg while on leave in the spring of 1944. Museums and art galleries in Britain's major cities had been emptied and their artefacts spirited away to the countryside for safekeeping. The National Galley in London, though denuded of exhibits, was the scene of the most defiant of cultural events. The redoubtable pianist Myra Hess decided the show must go on and held a series of classical concerts at the gallery. If bombs fell too close, she simply moved the audience, lock stock and barrel, to the basement. On 25th October 1944, Florence Foster Jenkins, a notoriously bad amateur soprano gave her only live performance at Carnegie Hall. She was later immortalised in an eponymous 2016 biopic starring Meryl Streep.

The National Gallery with Myra Hess

Gaslight

Directed by Thorold Dickinson
Starring Ingrid Bergman, Charles Boyer and Joseph Cotten
Premiered on the 4th May 1944

The film is based on a 1938 play by Nobel Prize winning author Patrick Hamilton. A famous opera singer is murdered in London, leaving behind no motive, no clues. Paula (Bergman), the young niece who discovered the body, is sent to Italy. She too studies music, until she elopes with an older, dashing pianist (Boyer). He convinces her to move back to the exact same house where her aunt was murdered. Soon her husband starts acting very strangely and starts convincing her that she is very ill and unable to go out. Trapped in the house alone with her husband, a somewhat-deaf cook, and a flirtatious housekeeper, Paula soon starts to hear noises, see and mislay things. Is she going mad? Or is her husband, who she has vowed to love, honour and obey, making her mad? Bergman steals the show and transforms the character of Paula Alquist from a weak, paranoid wimp of a wife into a woman struggling with her own identity and her role in marriage and society. Perhaps unintentionally, perhaps unwittingly, Bergman's Paula is a symbol and a superhero for all women trapped in an abusive marriage. The title of the film comes from a scene where Paula notices the gaslights dim of an evening and Boyer convinces her that it is a figment of her imagination. The film's enduring legacy is that it added the term 'gaslighting' to the English language.

To Have and Have Not

Directed by Howard Hawks
Starring Humphrey Bogart, Lauren Bacall and Walter Brennan
Released on 11th October 1944 in New York

The story, based very loosely on a 1937 Ernest Hemingway novel of the same name, is set in the Caribbean city of Fort de France, Martinique shortly after the fall of France to the Germans. Harry 'Steve' Morgan (Bogart) is a worldly wise fishing boat captain who is asked to smuggle people from a nearby island for the French Resistance. Initially very reluctant, Harry has to take on the job when a series of events leave him near financial ruin. Into his life comes Marie 'Slim' Browning (Bacall), an American pickpocket who has arrived on the island more by default than design. With his alcoholic pal in tow (Brennan) and the Gestapo breathing down his neck, Harry has a whole heap of issues suddenly making his once neutral and tranquil life explosive. Many critics have compared the movie unfavourably with the 1944 Oscar winner *Casablanca*, and there are many similarities. Both starred Bogart trying to make a living, reluctantly drawn into the war and both featured a complicated romantic affair. This film is probably best remembered for Slim's line: "If you want me, just whistle. You know how to whistle, don't you, Steve? You just put your lips together and blow." Bacall and Bogart married the following year and when Bogart died in 1956, Bacall placed a whistle in his coffin in homage to the line.

Desert Victory

Directed by Roy Boulting
Script by Frank Launder and Sidney Gillat
Academy award winner for Best Documentary Feature on 2nd March 1944

Desert Victory is a British documentary film that chronicles the Allies' efforts in the North African Campaign of World War II, specifically the Battle of El Alamein. The film opens with a map of North Africa and a voice-over explaining the strategic importance of the region and the objectives of the Allies. It then cuts to footage of the desert landscape with the troops preparing for battle, inter-cut with interviews with soldiers and commanders on the ground. The film documents the various stages of the battle, including the initial British advance, the counter attack by the Germans and the final Allied victory. Much of the footage was film captured from the retreating Germans which gives the movie an even-handed feel. One of the standout features of *Desert Victory* is the use of colour, which was relatively rare at the time. This added an extra level of realism to the film, allowing viewers to get a sense of the harsh desert conditions and the bravery of the soldiers on both sides. The film was a critical and commercial success upon its release and was widely praised for its authentic and unbiased portrayal of the conflict. It won several awards and is still considered one of the best and most balanced war documentaries of all time.

Arsenic and Old Lace

Directed by Frank Capra
Starring Cary Grant, Priscilla Lane and Raymond Massey
Based on a 1941 play by Joseph Kesselring of the same name

Released on the 1st September 1944 in New York City, the film saw Hollywood legend Cary Grant at his comedic and charming best. In it Mortimer Brewster (Grant), a New York critic of both drama and marriage, has finally married the girl next door Elaine Harper (Lane). But before heading off to Niagara Falls for the honeymoon, Mortimer stops in to see his aunts Abby and Martha Brewster. They are two sweet little old ladies who donate toys to charity and care for their nephew Teddy, a bugle blowing madman who thinks he's Theodore Roosevelt. But Abby and Martha aren't as nice and homely as they seem. Mortimer soon discovers, to his horror, that his dear old aunties have a dozen bodies buried in the basement. It seems the Brewster sisters have a hobby, namely luring lonely old men into their home and serving them elderberry wine laced with arsenic. To make matters worse, Mortimer's deranged and very dangerous brother Jonathan shows up. He is on the run from the law, has a dead body in the trunk of his car, a drunken plastic surgeon at his side and a face that looks like Frankenstein's monster. Mortimer frantically attempts to deal with dead bodies, insane asylum directors, attempted murders and a new bride all on a single crazy Halloween night. It is a movie that has stood the test of time and is funny to this day.

Casablanca

Directed by Michael Curtiz
Starring Humphrey Bogart, Ingrid Bergman and Paul Henreid
Winner of the Oscar for Outstanding Motion Picture on the 2nd March 1944

Set against the backdrop of the war, *Casablanca* was nominated for eight Academy Awards (Oscars) and won three in the categories Best Film, Best Director and Best Screenplay. The film stars screen icons Humphrey Bogart, in one of his more thoughtful roles, and Ingrid Bergman. Based on a stage play by Murray Burnett and Joan Alison, *Everyone Comes to Ricks*, it tells the story of a complicated love triangle with a heart-breaking ending. It ranks as one of the best movies of all time. The cinematography captures the atmosphere of the North African city of Casablanca, while the fast-paced story line fits in with the impending threat of conflict arriving on its doorstep. Sam the piano man in the bar played by Dooley Wilson, provides a moving soundtrack to the action. His rendition of the song *As Time Goes By* perfectly bookends the relationship between the two main characters. The film's makers, Warner Bros, threw all their best acting talent at the movie. Aside from the stars, the supporting cast included Peter Lorre, Sidney Greenstreet and Claude Rains. Casablanca is rated the ninth best American film of all time by BBC Culture and the second best movie by the American Film Institute, behind *Citizen Kane*.

Elsa Lanchester

Passport to Destiny

Directed by Ray McCary
Starring Elsa Lanchester and Gordon Oliver
Released on 25th February 1944

This is surely one of the most extraordinary films to have come out of America during the war and a candidate for the worst film ever made. It is also notable for being the only Hollywood movie in which Elsa Lanchester, best known as *The Bride of Frankenstein*, had the lead part and top billing. She plays a cockney charlady who is convinced she's protected by a 'lucky charm' once owned by her late husband (cut to a photo of her real life husband, Charles Laughton). With it she resolves to assassinate Hitler. During the London blitz, armed only with her bucket and a mop, she stows away on a ship across the English Channel and proceeds to scrub her way across Occupied Europe, pretending to be deaf and dumb. She lands up in Hitler's HQ in Berlin where language problems are solved by all the 'bad' Germans speaking English with strange guttural accents. Elsa gets a job as a cleaner in Hitler's office but he's out at the time so she delivers a propaganda-like speech to his empty chair. Some 'good' Germans opposed to Hitler (they all speak English with American accents) whisk Elsa back to England in a stolen plane. She is hailed as a heroine only to discover that the 'lucky charm' she took with her was part of a job-lot of glass eyes! The movie is dedicated to the fighting US forces overseas. One can only imagine what they made of it!

ITMA

Ran from 12th July 1939 to 6th January 1949
Number of series: 12
Number of episodes: 305 plus 5 specials

Created by the writing team of Tommy Handley, the star of the show and Ted Kavanagh, *Its That Man Again* (*ITMA*) got off to the most inauspicious of starts. Set on a pirate radio station on a ship where Handley himself chose the programmes, it featured characters such as a mad Russian and Cilly, his 'oh so silly' secretary. The show ran for four episodes and was not a great success.

When Hitler declared war on Britain, the BBC, scrabbling around for content, decided to award the comedy a run of 21 shows. A stalwart of British wartime radio was born. The setting for the new series was changed, as being set on a boat during a war was not credible. Instead Handley became Minister of Aggravation in the Ministry of Twerps. New characters were brought in including Funf, a German spy who satirised Nazi propaganda radio. The show was a success, perhaps not only because it lampooned the enemy, but possibly because it poked fun at the British government. This was too much for the BBC, and by series three the writers moved the setting to a run down seaside resort called *Foaming at the Mouth*. The show ran for twelve series until January 1949.

Caribbean Voices

Ran from 1943 to Spring 1958
Presented by Henry Swanzy
Produced by Una Marson

Caribbean Voices was a BBC radio programme created with the aim of showcasing the work of Caribbean poets, writers and playwrights. The first episode of *Caribbean Voices* was broadcast on 11th June 1943 and featured a reading of the short story *The Dawn Comes Up Like Thunder* by the Guyanese writer Edgar Mittelholzer.

The programme was initially broadcast on the BBC's Empire Service, which was heard by listeners in Africa, the Caribbean, and other parts of the British Empire. The programme was later picked up by the BBC's Home Service, which made it available to listeners in the United Kingdom. The programme was presented by Henry Swanzy, a Jamaican-born broadcaster who had a deep passion for Caribbean literature and culture. Swanzy was responsible for selecting the works that were featured on the programme and for introducing each episode with a commentary. *Caribbean Voices* was hugely popular and was credited with introducing many Caribbean writers to a wider audience. It featured some of the most well-known Caribbean authors such as George Lamming and Samuel Selvon (pictured) and was broadcast for over 15 years.

Wynford Vaughan-Thomas | War Correspondent

He was Britain's greatest war correspondent. Wherever our troops went, he went, risking his life to keep the people back home informed about the progress of the war. Here's an abridged dispatch from Italy in 1944:

"This is Wynford Vaughan-Thomas. Dispatch twenty-seven. Herbert Waldon's in his truck. He's got two microphones out, but no protection. So he'll record for as long as the bombs will let him. The first sounds of our own ack-ack and it's a sign that the usual night raid on our positions here is coming in. Right above us, the skies suddenly become as bright as day. The German flares are burning, hanging on us motionless overhead in the night sky and a shower of glittering silver lights coming down from them. Here on the ground, we feel as if we were standing under the flares on a fairground. Every tree, every house seems clearly little up. And our own flack is getting furious and fierce. [*Sound of gunfire*] And we've got guns all around us. Now they're sending up fierce flashes, stabbing into the night sky. And we can see the venomous puffs of our exploding shells clustering up above us there. The German aircraft are now right overhead. [*Sound of gunfire*]. Now everything on the ground is shooting, with vivid red tracers going criss-crossing, making an ever changing pattern all around us. But the Germans are pressing home their attack through it all. [*Sound of gunfire and aircraft*] The first bomb's going down. It's away to the left of us. And Walden's recording truck is now rocking on its springs" [*Aircraft sounds and gunfire*].

CBS Radio

Ed Murrow was the voice of American radio during the war. Much to the alarm of his bosses at CBS, he joined twenty five bombing raids over Germany, reporting back to the American public.

By the law of averages he should have died, but a superstition grew among airmen that if Murrow was aboard, you'd make it back safely. He was personally selected to read Supreme Commander Dwight D. Eisenhower's order of the day announcing the D-Day invasion and concluding: "We will accept nothing less than full victory. Good luck. And let us beseech the blessing of almighty God upon this great and noble undertaking." On D-Day, Murrow reluctantly agreed to stay behind to coordinate the first confused reports from CBS correspondents who came ashore at Utah Beach and Sword Beach. Reporter Charles Collingwood, lugging a 55-pound tape recorder, sent back the first eyewitness report to London: "The first craft onto the beaches was a little LCT (landing craft tank). They came in doggedly looking very small and gallant with their heads up. Offshore several miles loomed the silhouettes of the big ships. Although resistance was light", he continued, "this beach is still under considerable enemy gunfire. These boys are apparently having a pretty tough time in here on the beaches. It's not very pleasant." After D-Day, the Allied forces drove steadily through France toward Nazi Germany. Murrow joined the others on the Continent after Paris was liberated on 25th August 1944.

The Songs of War

Music was an essential part of the war effort, both comforting and motivating troops and civilians on both sides of the conflict. In the middle of the chaos and uncertainty of war, music offered relief whether it was songs that told stories of love and sorrow to patriotic music that inspired warriors. During 1944, radio was the main source of music as the vinyl needed to press records was requisitioned for the war effort. Here are some songs that were played on the radio to the armies on the front lines and to those back home:

Great Britain

Vera Lynn

Performed by the 'Forces' Sweetheart' Vera Lynn, *(There'll Be Bluebirds Over) The White Cliffs of Dover* symbolised the spirit of resilience and hope in the country throughout the hardship of war. The words of the song portrayed the famous Dover white cliffs as a representation of Britain and the promise of bluebirds soaring over them as a symbol of eventual victory against the Nazi forces. Both soldiers and civilians connected with the song's emotional lyrics and wistful melody, which offered a glimpse of a better future. Though bluebirds are not native to Britain, it is probable that the bluebirds in the song are the undercarriages of RAF planes reflected off the waters of the English Channel.

Noël Coward

Don't Let's Be Beastly To The Germans was Coward's most controversial song of the war. It contrasted to *London Pride* which was about the flowers that sprang up in bomb sites where Coward was his most poetic. It was a personal favourite of Prime Minister Winston Churchill. According to Sheridan Morley, Noël Coward's biographer, Churchill liked it so much that he asked for three reprises when Coward performed it on stage at a private party in the Haymarket Theatre. In his own words, Coward said that Churchill made him do it at least seven times in a single evening. Other members of the establishment interpreted it as being pro-German, and as a result it was quickly banned by the BBC.

Vera Lynn

Written at the onset of war in 1939, *We'll Meet Again* became the signature song of Vera Lynn. It is one of the most famous songs of the Second World War and resonated with soldiers going off to fight, as well as their families at home. The song gave its name to the 1943 musical film *We'll Meet Again* in which Vera Lynn played the lead role. Lynn's recording featured in the final scene of Stanley Kubrick's 1964 film *Dr. Strangelove*. During the Cold War, the song was included in a package of music and programmes by the BBC's Wartime Broadcasting Service to provide public information and morale-boosting broadcasts for 100 days after a nuclear attack.

The song *Kiss Me Goodbye, Sergeant Major*, written by Art Noel and Don Pelosi, perfectly captured the longing and loneliness felt by those left behind. The lyrics showed an anxious wife or sweetheart anticipating her soldier's safe return and a warm welcome. Both soldiers and civilians loved it because of the catchy music and heartfelt lyrics, which served as a reassuring reminder of the love and support waiting for them at home.

United States of America

The Golden Gate Quartet (here pictured in 1964)

A cheerful song that became well-known during World War II was *Stalin wasn't Stallin'.* The song, sung by the American gospel group the Golden Gate Quartet, poked fun at Hitler and Mussolini while expressing admiration for the Soviet Union and its leader Joseph Stalin by using creative wordplay and catchy rhymes. The song's light-hearted attitude belied how serious the conflict was. Many Americans, who viewed the Soviet Union as a vital partner in the combat against fascism, found its message of support for the Soviet Union to be moving.

The Andrews Sisters

Don Raye and Hughie Prince composed the well-known World War II song *Boogie Woogie Bugle Boy* for the military musical comedy *Buck Privates*, which went on to become one of the most popular movies of the war. The song was initially written for Lou Costello, but it was immediately reworked for the harmonic vocals of The Andrews Sisters who sang four songs in the movie. It recalls the tale of a trumpet player who was drafted into the American Army and was forced to play nothing except the Reveille, a trumpet call that is used to awaken military men at dawn, in place of his favoured jazz numbers.

The song *Praise the Lord and Pass the Ammunition* became well-known during the war. The song takes its title from the words that a Navy chaplain supposedly uttered during the attack on Pearl Harbor, urging troops to keep fighting despite overwhelming odds. With a chorus urging soldiers to "keep those fighting words alight", the lyrics portrayed a spirit of resolve and faith in the face of difficulty.

Russia

Mark Bernes

Dark is the Night is a Soviet song associated with the Great Patriotic War (WWII). It was originally performed by Mark Bernes in the 1943 war film *Two Soldiers*. The song was composed by Nikita Bogoslovsky and lyrics by Vladimir Agatov specifically for the film. The song is a gentle, lyrical ballad that expresses a feeling of homesickness and devotion to one's loved ones. Despite official accusations of being a 'Philistine' sentimental tune, it became a symbol of the war years for millions of Soviet people. It stands in contrast to the typical war songs, which were field marching songs or civil patriotic ones.

The song's *Katyusha's* eerie tune and haunting lyrics addressed the suffering and longing of those torn apart by conflict, yet its upbeat chorus inspired soldiers to fight on. It was so popular it became an unofficial anthem of the Soviet Union. The song serves as a bittersweet recollection of a period when music could bring a country together in the face of hardship. It tells the story a Russian woman called *Katyusha*. Standing on a steep riverbank, she sings a song to her beloved, a soldier serving far away. The theme of the song is that the soldier will protect the Motherland and its people while his grateful girl will keep and protect their love. The name *Katyusha* had a double meaning for Russian soldiers. Literally 'Little Kate', it could both refer to the 'girl back home' or the fearsome *Katyusha* multiple rocket launchers, Russia's most deadly weapon of the war.

Germany

A well-known German military song from World War II called *Panzerlied* (Tank Song) praised the bravery and camaraderie of the men serving their country. The rousing chorus and driving melody were meant to embolden soldiers on the front lines and instil pride in their sacrifice. Although the song's lyrics did not specifically mention Nazi philosophy or the tragedies of the war, its affiliation with the German Wehrmacht has made it a controversial work of music in the decades since the war. Today, *Panzerlied* stands as a reminder of the ability of music to arouse feelings and inspire allegiance, even during a terrible and morally challenging battle.

Marlene Dietrich

Originally German but universal, *Lili Marlene* was the 20th century's most popular soldier's song. It started as a German WW1 poem, and was set to music in the 1930s. It is a simple song with a haunting melody, and in common with many songs of the era tells a story of a yearning for 'The girl back home'. The Nazi propaganda machine decided that playing an English language version to Allied troops would somehow weaken their resolve. However, the opposite was true and Allied forces took it to their hearts. It came to embody the commonality of all soldiers' experience. There were even reports of impromptu ceasefires between otherwise bitter enemies, when it came on the radio. German Propaganda Minister Goebbels came to hate the song and sought to have it banned. Marlene Dietrich sang versions in both English and German.

Italy

The Italian folk song *Bella Ciao* was used as a resistance anthem in World War II. Although its exact roots are unknown, it is thought that farm workers who were toiling in the fields of northern Italy first sang it. It was quickly adopted by anti-fascist partisans who fought the Germans and their Italian allies during the war. With a chorus that encouraged listeners to "stand up and join the struggle", the song's lyrics portrayed a wish for freedom and a desire to oppose oppression.

France

Le Chant des Partisans (The Partisans' Song), a song from the French Resistance, symbolised the spirit of defiance and resistance against German occupation. The song's strong words and eerie rhythm showed a spirit of strength and hope during unfathomable tragedy, with a chorus that firmly pushed listeners to "pick up arms, citizens". It provided the French Resistance with a vision of a free and democratic France that was worth fighting for. The song serves as a permanent reminder of the bravery and sacrifice of those who fought Nazism as well as the enduring power of music to inspire and bring people together in the quest for a better society.

Henry Wood's 'Last' Last Night of the Proms

Sir Henry Wood in 1900

Founder and chief conductor of the Proms for nearly 50 years, Henry Wood was just 26 when he put on and conducted the first 'Prom' concert, held at Queen's Hall on 10th August 1895. Wood and co-founder Robert Newman had a vision for a series of concerts that anyone could attend, regardless of how much money they earned. In 1895, Promming (standing) tickets to these concerts cost just a shilling. Wood and Newman wanted to introduce a broad range of classical music to a much wider audience, always working to truly democratise music that was seen as high-brow. The atmosphere of the concerts was always informal; people were permitted to eat and drink during performances (providing they kept the noise down during the quiet pieces) and the music had to be popular. In the first seasons, a tradition was established of a 'Wagner Night' on Mondays and a 'Beethoven Night' on Fridays. As the seasons went on, Wood continually presented an enterprising mixture of the familiar and the adventurous, programming new works each season. By 1920, Wood had introduced many of the leading composers of the day to the Proms audiences, including Richard Strauss, Debussy, Rachmaninov, Ravel and Vaughan Williams. Henry Wood was passionate about promoting young and talented performers. He fought to raise orchestral standards, abolishing the system in which orchestral players could send deputies to rehearsals and appear in person only for the concert. Wood passed away on the 19th August 1944 aged 75, having conducted at the Proms for nearly half a century. After his death, the concerts were officially renamed as the 'Henry Wood Promenade Concerts'. They continue to be the longest running series of orchestral concerts in the world. Today Henry Wood is remembered every year at the Proms with the placing of a bronze bust, borrowed from the Royal Academy of Music, at the back of the Royal Albert Hall's stage. On the Last Night of the Proms each year, a member of the audience places a chaplet over the bust as Wood's *Fantasia on British Sea Songs* is performed. On the 10th June 1944, the first night of the The Proms opened with *Overture Le Carnaval Romain* by Hector Berlioz and finished with Elgar's *Pomp and Circumstance March No. 1 in D major, Land of Hope and Glory*. The season finished on the 12th August, opening with Richard Wagner's *The Mastersingers of Nuremberg* and closing with a rousing rendition of *God Save the King*. Prom 29, scheduled to take place on 13th July was cancelled by the authorities due to flying 'Doodlebug' bombs, which had started to fall on London in June 1944. However, it was decided to resume the concerts the following day as the Royal Albert Hall was a sturdy building able to withstand a direct hit. That Wood continued to play all classical music, regardless of its country of birth of the composer, is testament to his love of music and was in sharp contrast to the attitude of Nazi Germany who banned foreign 'decadent' music.

The Royal Albert Hall in London

Alun Lewis | 1915-1944

Alun Lewis

Alun Lewis was born in the Welsh town of Cwmaman. Before the war, he was a journalist, poet, and short-story writer. Despite his pacifist beliefs, he volunteered in the army in 1940 as a Sapper in the Royal Engineers. He served in the East before a commission in the infantry in 1943. He died of a shotgun wound in the Arakan front in Burma on the 5th March 1944. He wrote this poem while stationed with the Royal Engineers at Longmoor, Hampshire.

All Day It Has Rained

Written by Alun Lewis

All day it has rained, and we on the edge of the moors
Have sprawled in our bell-tents, moody and dull as boors,
Groundsheets and blankets spread on the muddy ground
And from the first grey wakening we have found
No refuge from the skirmishing fine rain
And the wind that made the canvas heave and flap
And the taut wet guy-ropes ravel out and snap.
All day the rain has glided, wave and mist and dream,
Drenching the gorse and heather, a gossamer stream
Too light to stir the acorns that suddenly
Snatched from their cups by the wild south-westerly
Pattered against the tent and our upturned dreaming faces.
And we stretched out, unbuttoning our braces,
Smoking a Woodbine, darning dirty socks,
Reading the Sunday papers - I saw a fox
And mentioned it in the note I scribbled home; -
And we talked of girls and dropping bombs on Rome,
And thought of the quiet dead and the loud celebrities
Exhorting us to slaughter, and the herded refugees;
As of ourselves or those whom we
For years have loved, and will again
Tomorrow maybe love; but now it is the rain
Possesses us entirely, the twilight and the rain.
And I can remember nothing dearer or more to my heart
Than the children I watched in the woods on Saturday
Shaking down burning chestnuts for the schoolyard's merry play,
Or the shaggy patient dog who followed me
By Sheet and Steep and up the wooded scree
To the Shoulder o' Mutton where Edward Thomas brooded long
On death and beauty - till a bullet stopped his song.

Fair Stood the Wind for France

Author: H.E. Bates   First Edition Published: 1944

Set in occupied France during the Second World War, this book was written while the war was still taking place. This adds an additional dimension of tension to an already suspenseful story. It begins when the main protagonist John Franklin, a young British airman, realises that his plane has malfunctioned forcing him to bring it down in a field in Nazi occupied France. Franklin and his crew make it to a farmhouse in the countryside where they are hidden and kept safe. They hope that false papers can be obtained in order for them to be smuggled back to England. Meanwhile, Franklin falls in love with the beautiful young daughter of the farmer. Even though the rest of the story follows fairly predictable lines, Bates does what Bates does best by focusing on what it was like for ordinary people who were living their lives as best they could despite the horrors of war.

Towards Zero (the last novel in the Superintendent Battle series)

Author: Agatha Christie   Published: June 1944

The story jumps straight into classic Christie fare: a large number of people are gathered together for an unimportant reason. Some of them obviously have pre-existing histories with each other; some of them we are led to believe are meeting for the first time and, of course, not everybody is necessarily who they claim to be. The zero in the title is the time of the murder. The events and reasons that lead up to this point are as important as the murder itself. It has all the teasers and all the fantastic suspects we love with all the twists and turns. All the suspects are briefly caught in the spotlight of suspicion before the story moves on. Superintendent Battle is a 'non-detective' in this story. He barely influences the resolution at all. The crime is actually wrapped up by a random passer-by who happens to be in the area for a totally unconnected reason. It was as if Christie had fallen out of love with Battle; she would not write about him again.

A Haunted House and Other Short Stories

Author: Virginia Woolf   Publication Date: January 1944

This collection of short stories was published three years after the author's death. The tales in the book reflect Virginia Woolf's experimental writing style, acting as an enlightening introduction to the longer fiction of this pioneer novelist. It collects some of the best shorter fiction of one of the most important writers of our time. In most stories, her interest is clearly in searching for the truth about the characters through their inner monologue or the narrator's interpretations of their exterior clues. The end result is not always as expected, as in *An Unwritten Novel* or *Moments of Being*. Elsewhere in the book, the stories explore the puzzles that surround us. From something as simple and trivial as an unusually positioned dot on the wall in *The Mark on the Wall*, to the consequences of our life choices, such as marriage, as uncovered in the brilliantly imaginative story *Lappin and Lapinova*.

The Lost Weekend

Author: Charles R. Jackson   First Published: 1944

The book chronicles five days and nights in the life of Don Birnam, an alcoholic writer who we follow on his 'lost weekend' of binge drinking and frantic search for money. Things quickly spiral out of control for Don as the number of chaotic incidents and dramatic events grow page after page to a relentlessly dramatic crescendo. Don is far from being a lovable character. He's not looking for redemption and seems to have no intention to stop drinking. His periods of sobriety are only short brackets between other lost days and wild drunken sprees. There is something raw and honest in his personality though, that ultimately make the reader care for him. Billy Wilder directed a film adaptation of the book in 1945. It starred Ray Miland. Although diverting from the novel in some crucial elements (e.g. Don's homosexuality, that is completely disregarded in the movie), the film is equally uncompromising and sincere.

The Razor's Edge

Author: W. Somerset Maugham   First Published: 1944

Maugham inserts himself into the narrative which seems to work well with his being the storyteller and also a character in the book. He is the writer of Larry Darrell's story as he befriends both him and his friends. Larry's story is told through the lens of his friends who have recognised a drastic change in his personality since returning from WW1 where he served as a fighter pilot. Larry is a much more subdued and introspective man now that he has witnessed death. Living a 'normal' lifestyle is futile to him as he seems to be grappling with what life should really be about. His friends and his fiancée think he should be making lots of money and working his way up the corporate ladder, moving on with his life and finding meaning through his work and his relationships. But this lifestyle of conforming to the expectations of society will not suit Larry. This is not his definition of happiness.

Anna and The King of Siam

Author: Margaret Landon   First Published: 1944

Anna Leonowens, an Anglo-Indian, was an unlikely candidate to change the course of Siamese (Thai) history. A young widow and mother, her services were engaged in the 1860's by King Mongkut of Siam to help him communicate with foreign governments and be the tutor to his children. Stepping off the steamer from London, Anna found herself in an exotic land she could have only dreamed of. A lush landscape of mystic faiths and curious people along with a King's palace bustling with royal pageantry, ancient custom, and harems. One of her pupils, the young prince Chulalongkorn, was particularly influenced by Leonowens and her Western ideals. He learns about Abraham Lincoln and the tenets of democracy from her. Years later he would become Siam's most progressive King. Weaving meticulously researched facts with beautifully imagined scenes, Margret Landon recreates an unforgettable portrait of life in a forgotten exotic land.

Mother Goose

Author: Tasha Tudor   **First Published:** 1944

Mother Goose was a reworking of *The Real Mother Goose*, a 1916 work by Blanche Fisher Wright. It follows the same format of nursery rhymes all accompanied by illustrations. In this book there are seventy-seven. The rhymes include classics such as *Hickory Dickory Dock*, *Humpty Dumpty*, *Little Miss Muffet* and some other not so well known rhymes for children. The book's timeless, beloved rhymes stand out as its greatest strength. Complementing these are vivid illustrations, each page adorned with either colourful watercolour paintings or evocative black-and-white pencil sketches. These charming visuals beautifully depict children, farm life, animals, and nature. However, the book does show its age in certain aspects, particularly in its language, with some vocabulary feeling less familiar in modern times. There's also a line that reads, "She whipped them all soundly and put them to bed." Thankfully, times have changed.

The Wind On The Moon

Author: Eric Linklater   **Publication Date:** 1944

In the English village of Midmeddlecum, Major Palfrey asks his two daughters to behave themselves while he is off at war. Sighs Dinah: "I think that we are quite likely to be bad, however hard we try not to be". Her sister Dorinda adds helpfully: "Very often, when we think we are behaving well, some grown-up person says we are really quite bad. It's difficult to tell which is which", and so the fun begins. The book is comparable to *Alice in Wonderland*. Both create fictional and impossible worlds to reveal a great deal about our own world when explored by headstrong female juvenile leads. Both take time to make philosophical observations about our own world. One of the main themes is freedom and confinement, both in terms of imprisonment (often false imprisonment) and independence of thought and action. Like all good philosophy books, it asks more than it answers.

Eskimo Boy (Ivik: den Faderløse - 'Ivik the Fatherless' in Danish)

Author: Pipaluk Freuchen   **Published:** 1944

Freuchen was born to a Danish explorer father and an Inuit mother who died young. In 1944, Pipaluk, and her father escaped Nazi Occupied Denmark for Sweden. Her book *Eskimo Boy* can be seen as semi-autobiographical as it deals with both loss and survival. In the book, Ivik's father is killed by a walrus while on a hunting trip. Ivik then has to save his family from starvation. After several scrapes with danger, Ivik ends up killing a polar bear thereby saving his family. Reviewing the book, the Lexington Herald described it as "permeated with the spirit of Eskimo culture". While the Manchester Guardian described the book as "a little masterpiece of writing". The Swedish edition was illustrated by Freuchen's cousin Ingrid Vang Nyman, she of *Pippi Longstocking* fame. The book is of its time; it is hard to see a story which ends happily with the slaying of a polar bear being successful today.

Britain entered the global theatre of war over 80 years ago. The conflict affected every aspect of life at home, including theatre. While the last few months of 1939 might have felt like a 'Phoney War' to some, they had a very real impact on the theatre business as the government ordered the immediate closure of venues over safety fears. Equity, the actors' trade union, urged that work in theatre should be regarded as National Service for all artists either over military age or unfit to serve. However, that depended on plays being staged. The nationwide closure meant thousands became unemployed overnight, with those in touring companies stranded miles from home. It took a concerted campaign, including a public intervention by Irish playwright George Bernard Shaw who called the measure "a masterstroke

George Bernard Shaw

of unimaginative stupidity", for the decision to be reversed and for places of entertainment to start the morale-boosting business of entertaining once more. When in February 1943 the group submitted a motion "believing this to be in the best interests of the British public under present conditions and of the theatrical profession as a whole", it attracted 200 signatories including Laurence Olivier, John Gielgud, Hermione Gingold, Vivien Leigh, Beatrice Lillie and John Mills. War work meant more people at home had money in their pockets. In many places, theatres reaped the rewards of this new disposable income with the public desiring to forget the fighting for a few hours. Anecdotal evidence from the Walter Hudd Company, a troupe lead by thespian Frederick Walter Hudd, suggested wartime audiences appreciated plays including *She Stoops To Conquer*, *Hedda Gabler* and Shaw's *Man Of Destiny*. However, conflict didn't crush contemporary creativity. A number of new plays were written and premiered during the war, including

Vivien Leigh

Coward's *Blithe Spirit*, *Present Laughter* and *This Happy Breed*, Terence Rattigan's *Flare Path* and *While the Sun Shines*, and works by Agatha Christie, Esther McCracken and Philip King among others. While wartime conditions proved challenging for the theatre, they were also a time of opportunity and creativity; something that continued after 1945. Following the end of hostilities, long-discussed plans for a National Theatre would be resurrected and finally acted upon. The Council for the Encouragement of Music and the Arts (CEMA), founded in 1940, morphed into the Arts Council providing continued state support for the arts. Plays that saw their debut in 1944 included Tennessee Williams' *Glass Menagerie* and Mary Chase's *Harvey*, a play about a man with an imaginary friend rabbit that was made in to a film starring James Stewart in 1950. 1944 also saw George Bernard Shaw's *The British Party System*, a satire on British politics.

Tennessee Williams

Blithe Spirit

Written by Noël Coward
Premiered on the 16th June 1941 at the Manchester Opera House
Resident throughout 1944 at the Duchess Theatre in the West End

Noël Coward

The comic play, described by Coward as a comedic farce in three acts, sees socialite and novelist Charles Condomine inviting a medium, Madame Arcati, to his home to conduct a séance for research on his next book. However, the plan goes awry when Charles's deceased first wife, Elvira, begins to haunt him and disrupt his current marriage to his second wife, Ruth, who cannot perceive the ghost. The title of the play is taken from Shelley's poem *To A Skylark* which includes the line "*Hail to thee, blithe spirit! Bird thou never wert.*" The idea originated after Coward's London office and apartment were destroyed during the Blitz. To escape London, he took a brief holiday with actress Joyce Carey in Portmeirion in Wales. Coward recalled: "We sat on the beach with our backs against the sea wall and discussed my idea for a comedy play about ghosts for several hours." He then worked relentlessly for six days until the play was finished claiming "...with disdaining archness and false modesty, I will admit that I knew it was witty, I knew it was well constructed, and I also knew that it would be a success." He was right. It has been staged ever since, including a recent screen adaptation in the 2020 film starring Dan Stevens and Dame Judi Dench.

Henry V
A film adaptation partly funded by the British Government

Laurence Olivier

This film precisely met the requirement to raise the moral of Britain during the Second World War; it is both cheering and inspiring. However, it is more than just patriotic propaganda. *Henry V* is an excellent beginning to Olivier's series of Shakespearean films. This adaptation, the first Shakespeare play to be filmed in colour, is poetry within the historical context of English patriotic pageantry. At the outset, we are asked to imagine "a kingdom for a stage, princes to act and monarchs to behold the swelling scene." The film begins in the enclosed intimacy of a studio-recreation of the Globe Theatre, performed before an appropriately attired Elizabethan audience. However, Olivier then uses the medium of cinema to physically 'open up' the play as it develops from scene to scene, increasingly taking advantage of more elaborate studio scenery. This ultimately leads to staging the climactic Battle of Agincourt using vast exterior locations. As a director, Olivier transforms the conventions of the stage. He shows us a fleet of miniature warships engulfed in English Channel fog and the Chorus (played by Leslie Banks) superimposed against painted, moving backdrops. Towards the end, we see the bleak French post-battle countryside; a zone of pillage, poverty and heartbreak in the aftermath of battle. This version of *Henry V* was made with a wartime audience in mind. The 'V' in the title is a perfect symbolic reference for the times. Here, the overconfident Dauphin (Max Adrian) and other French nobles stand in for authoritarianism whilst the common men who make up the motley army of British archers and infantry represent their enemy, and ultimately the victors.

The Glass Menagerie

The Glass Menagerie

Written by Tennessee Williams
Premiered in Chicago 1944
Starring Laurette Taylor, Eddie Dowling, Julie Haydon and Anthony Ross

The Glass Menagerie is a one-act play first produced in 1944, and laid down in book form in 1945. The play launched Williams' career and is considered by many critics to be his finest work. In it, Amanda Wingfield lives in a tenement in St. Louis, Missouri clinging to the myth of her early years as a Southern Belle, repeating stories of romantic escapades to her two children. Her daughter Laura, who wears a leg brace, is painfully shy and seeks solace in her collection of glass animals. Amanda's son Tom, through whose memory the action is seen, is desperate to escape his stifling home life and drab warehouse job. Amanda encourages him to bring "gentleman callers" home to his sister. When Tom brings Jim O'Connor for dinner, Amanda believes that her prayers have been answered. Laura blossoms during Jim's visit, flattered by his attention. After kissing her, however, Jim confesses that he is engaged to be married. Laura retreats to her shell and Amanda blames Tom, who leaves home for good after a final fight with his mother. This work along with *A Streetcar Named Desire* (1947), *Cat on a Hot Tin Roof* (1955), *Sweet Bird of Youth* (1959) and *The Night of the Iguana* (1961), propelled Williams into the pantheon of great American playwrights of the twentieth century alongside Arthur Miller and Eugene O'Neill.

Noele Gordon
credit: The Noele Gordon Archive

The Lisbon Story

Written by Harold Purcell, Music by Harry Parr-Davies
Premiered on 31st May 1943
Resident until 8th July 1944 at the London Hippodrome in the West End

The Lisbon Story is a 1943 British musical. The story is a wartime espionage thriller set in the cities of Lisbon and Paris during the summer of 1942. The story revolves around a Parisian singing star, Gabrielle Girard, and British Foreign Office agent David Warren. They meet in Lisbon, a neutral city in WWII, where David and his co-agent are caring for Lisette Sargon. Her scientist father is captured by Nazis, but Gabrielle helps secure his release and reunite him with Lisette. However, a Nazi representative threatens to reveal their secrets unless Gabrielle becomes his mistress. David and Mike attempt to smuggle them to London, using a patriotic musical performance as a diversion. The story ends with gunfire and bombs as they make their escape. Amongst the cast was a young Noele Gordon, who would go on to reach iconic status as Meg Mortimer in the soap opera *Crossroads*. The show was a big hit and ran for over a year at the London Hippodrome. In 1946, the musical was adapted as a film with several actors reprising their roles from the stage. The song, *Pedro the Fisherman*, became a hit and was subsequently recorded by many artists including Gracie Fields and Julie Andrews.

Yasuo Kuniyoshi

In 1906, 16-year-old Yasuo Kuniyoshi came to the USA alone from Japan. He made his name as a painter, and aged 40, his work was shown at the Museum of Modern Art in New York. But there was one thing Kuniyoshi longed for that he was always denied: American citizenship. In fact, he was classified as an 'enemy alien' during World War II. He wasn't sent to an internment camp like most West Coast Japanese were, but there were restrictions. His camera was taken away from him, his binoculars seized and his bank account was frozen.

However, Kuniyoshi was deeply patriotic and devoted to America. So when the Department of Defense asked him to do some drawings for propaganda posters, he was eager to help. He sketched a mother and child hanging from a tree as a Japanese soldier leaves the scene. In *Clean Up This Mess*, a woman's hand discards a bag filled with Japanese symbols, like a flag and a samurai sword. The posters never got made, but the anti-Japanese sentiment was clear. It must have been difficult for Kuniyoshi to repudiate his roots. Abstract expressionism and newer movements nudged him off the art scene after he died in 1953. The photograph above shows Kuniyoshi in his studio, at 30 East Fourteenth St. in New York, photographed for the Federal Art Project Photographic Division. Kuniyoshi is working on his painting *Upside Down Table and Mask*.

Trafalgar Square by Piet Mondrian

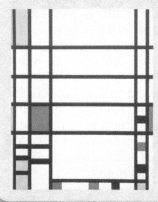

Pieter Cornelis Mondrian was a Dutch painter and art theorist who is considered one of the greatest artists of the 20th century. His work influenced not only the course of abstract painting and numerous major styles and art movements, but also fields outside the domain of painting such as design, architecture and fashion. *Trafalgar Square* was a painting that Mondrian started in 1939 whilst living in London, having left Paris a year earlier over fears of a German invasion. In 1940, Mondrian then moved to America. Overall he worked on the painting for 4 years until 1943, when he applied the finishing touches whilst living in New York. Mondrian died of pneumonia on 1st February 1944 and was interred at the Cypress Hill Cemetery in Brooklyn, New York, USA.

The Harvard Mark I

Closeup of an input/output reader

The Harvard Mark I was also known as the IBM Automatic Sequence Controlled Calculator (ASCC). It was one of the earliest electromechanical computers. At 51 feet long, it was enormous. It used 765,000 electromechanical components, hundreds of miles of wire and weighed over 4 tonnes. Conceived in 1937 by Howard Aiken, the design built on Charles Babbage's Analytical Engine which was proposed some 100 years earlier. It was built in IBM's Endicott plant in Broome County, New York then shipped to Harvard in February 1944. Capable of running instructions coded onto punched paper tape, it could carry out calculations automatically. One of the first programs run on the machines was by John von Neumann whilst working on the Manhatten project. He needed to see if implosion was a realistic option for detonating the atomic bomb that would be detonated a year later. Although it was not the first operational computer, it was the first to automate the execution of complex calculations, marking a significant advance in computing. Aiken would go on to build three further versions of the machine resulting in the Mark IV in 1952 which was an all-electronic device to be used by the US Air Force.

The Tide Predicting Machine that altered the D-Day Landings

Mechanical tide predicting machine

The first tide predicting machine was invented by British mathematician Sir William Thomson in 1872. He would later become the 1st Baron Kelvin, with the unit of absolute temperature named in his honour. The complex analogue mechanical computer could be used to predict tides based on harmonic analysis of tidal patterns. In World War II, Scottish-born Group Captain James Martin Stagg of the Royal Air Force was appointed Chief Meteorological Officer for Operation Overlord, the code-name for the Battle of Normandy. The plan for the Normandy Landings (Operation Neptune) required precise forecasting of the tides in order to ensure ground troops landed on the beaches between low and mid tide. This would minimise the risk from German defences buried in the sand along the coast. General Dwight D. Eisenhower had tentatively earmarked the 5th June as D-Day. However the day before, Group Captain Stagg met with Eisenhower to present a forecast suggesting the 5th June was too stormy with an unfavourable tide. He predicted a small weather window on the 6th June. This information proved vital, so the operation was put back by 24 hours.

The Mass Production of Penicillin

Alexander Fleming in his lab in 1943

Scottish physician Alexander Fleming discovered penicillin in 1928. However, it was not widely used at first due to the difficulty of producing it in volume. In 1942, Harry Lambert was successfully treated with pure penicillin for a fatal infection of the nervous system (streptococcal meningitis). He was cured in a week. This breakthrough led the British War Cabinet to set up the Penicillin Committee, which would oversee projects for mass production. Efforts by scientists in companies both in the US and UK were coordinated to develop a process for large scale production. It was the US-based Pfizer scientist Jasper H. Kane who proposed a deep-tank fermentation method suitable for producing large volumes of pharmaceutical-grade penicillin that came as the breakthrough. Production facilities were opened in 1944 and an enormous effort saw more than 2.3 million doses produced ahead of the Normandy landings. It became known as the 'Wonder Drug' and is reputed to have saved the lives of 12-15% of all the casualties. Alexander Fleming was knighted in 1944 and would be awarded the Nobel prize in Physiology or Medicine in 1945.

Combating Sunburn : 'The Self-Inflicted Wound'

US Army Sun Cream

Sunburn was a serious issue for troops in World War II with so many serving in North Africa, the Mediterranean, and the Pacific. A soldier recovering from sunburn would typically miss 5 days from the battlefield. The US Army recorded 15,000 cases of sunburn on their casualty lists. It was such a problem that the British Army treated sunburn as "a self-inflicted wound", with every case receiving punishment. In the US marines, some men were docked as much as 5 days pay for "abuse of government property". Many soldiers therefore suffered their sunburn agony in silence. In 1944, a US airmen named Benjamin Green patented his Red Vet Pet (red veterinary petrolatum). It was a sticky, bright red gel-like petroleum jelly which offered some sun protection. However it was not widely circulated. After the war, he became a pharmacist and commercialised his product under the name Coppertone. In 1946, Austrian scientist Franz Greiter invented Gletscher Crème (Glacier Cream), which later became the foundation for the company Piz Buin. It was named after the mountain where Greiter purportedly got sunburned.

Hobart's Funnies

Hobart's Funnies were a remarkable array of specialised armoured vehicles developed by British engineer Major General Percy Hobart to address the unique challenges of amphibious landings and advancement in light of the disastrous Dieppe raid of 1942. Deployed primarily during the Normandy landings on D-Day in June 1944, Hobart's Funnies played a pivotal role in the success of Operation Overlord. Most vehicles were adapted from Churchill or M4 Sherman tanks. Among the notable vehicles were the Churchill AVRE (Armoured Vehicle Royal Engineers), equipped with a massive 290mm petard mortar for demolishing obstacles and bunkers. There was also the Sherman Crab, a tank fitted with a rotating flail drum to clear minefields. The DD (Duplex Drive) tanks, nicknamed Donald Duck tanks, had large watertight canvases and secondary propellers. This meant they could be launched at sea, then lower their flotation screens once they had reached land to fight as an ordinary tank. Perhaps the most iconic of Hobart's Funnies was the Churchill Crocodile, a flame-throwing tank that could unleash a torrent of fire onto enemy positions, making it highly effective in clearing out fortified emplacements.

An AVRE with petard mortar

The DD amphibious tank

Churchill Crocodile with flame-thrower

Britain's First Operational Jet Fighter

The British had been working on jet technology since the 1930s, led by the pioneering work of RAF Officer Frank Whittle. The first British jet to fly was the Gloster E.28/39 prototype on the 15th May 1941. This led to the manufacture of the Gloster Meteor, the first operational military jet fighter. Although it was prone to stability issues at high speeds due to poor aerodynamics, it was still an important milestone in aviation history.

A pair of F.3 Gloster Meteors patrolling the skies

The Meteors were first deployed with No. 616 Squadron at RAF Manston in 1944, briefed to seek out and destroy incoming German V-1 rockets. The first operational sortie was on the 27th July 1944. The first successes were on the 4th August 1944 when two V-1's were downed. However, the unproven Meteor was unreliable. In the last two weeks of August, three of them were written off in non-combat incidents. As the Meteor's were slower and less heavily armed than the Messerschmitt Me 262 jet, they saw limited wartime duties. In 1946, the F.4 variant of the Meteor became the first civilian-registered jet aircraft in the world.

Mulberry harbours

The German 'Atlantic Wall' of fortifications protecting the European coastline from Allied invasion had proven almost impenetrable. The failed attempt to capture the port of Dieppe in 1942 provided a graphic demonstration. For a successful coastal invasion, the Allies would require huge amounts of heavy equipment and supplies to be landed by large ocean going ships, requiring deep water jetties and a harbour. With little prospect of capturing an existing heavily defended port, the Allies developed an ingenious solution of creating two temporary, portable harbours that could be towed across the Channel and rapidly installed as part of the D-Day landings. Built in secret over the course of a year, the harbours consisted of 212 Phoenix caissons (concrete boxes) which were sunk when in situ. Old ships were also deliberately scuttled to create breakwaters. The harbours were then completed with a network of floating pontoons, roadways and piers. Mulberry "A" was built off Omaha beach whilst Mulberry "B" was sited off Gold Beach. Mulberry "B" was built successfully and used for 10 months allowing for some 2.5 million men, 500,000 vehicles and 4 million tons of supplies to be landed. Unfortunately the partially built Mulberry "A" was destroyed beyond repair during a violent storm on the 19th June, so was never used.

Old ships used as breakwaters

Installed Caissons with gun turrets

Aerial view of Mulberry "B" harbour

Airborne Lifeboats

Rescuing aircrew who ditched in the sea was tricky, especially if they were near enemy-held territory. If rescue by seaplane or high speed launch was not possible, the best the stranded airmen could hope for was an inflatable rubber dinghy dropped by an allied aircraft. However, these dinghys were vulnerable to winds and tides propelling them to shore resulting in eventual capture. The ingenious solution was the development of a 32-foot wooden hulled, powered lifeboat that could be dropped from a specially modified heavy bomber such as the Avro Lancaster or Vickers Warwick. The boats were dropped from 700 feet with their descent slowed

An Uffa Fox airborne lifeboat in front of a modified Vickers Warwick

by six parachutes. The boats were designed for self-righting if they landed upside down. With two x 4hp motors and an auxiliary mast and sails, the lifeboats carried emergency equipment including waterproof suits, food, medical supplies and a radio. The lifeboats were successfully used to save airmen in September 1944 as part of Operation Market Garden.

The Higgins Boat

The Landing Craft Vehicle Personnel (LCVP), otherwise known as a Higgins Boat, was an amphibious landing boat used extensively in World War 2 most notably in the D-Day landings. Designed in the 1930's by American businessman Andrew Higgins, these shallow-draft, barge-like boats were originally sold to trappers and oil drillers for use in swamps and marshes. In 1939, the US military compared the Higgins boat to other designs and found it outperformed them for amphibious landings. The 36-foot long, 11-foot wide boat could carry up to a 36-man platoon or a mix of troops, vehicles and cargo. A version was sold to the British army where it was known as an 'R-boat' and used in commando raids. Many Higgins boats were used in the 1944 Normandy landings as well as many other theatres of war around world. Troops would typically enter the boat by climbing down a cargo net from a troop ship. It would then be driven to shore where the steel ramp at the front would be lowered allowing swift disembarkation. They did have their limitations as they were vulnerable to enemy fire due to being only lightly armoured. They could also get stuck over reefs or in very shallow water. This led to the development of tracked landing boats which could drive up the beach.

Troops boarding from a cargo net

An LCVP with packed with troops

Wading ashore at Omaha Beach

The Judas Goat

The USAAF developed a tactical flying formation known as a combat box to protect their vulnerable heavy bombers from attack from enemy fighters. This staggered formation, much like a flock of geese, required a lead aircraft to direct the group. The difficulty in forming these bombing raids was that it needed to be done under radio silence, so not to tip off the Germans. In addition, bomber formations

'First Seargant' - a Consolidated B-24D assembly ship

would typically comprise aircraft joining from different airfields. The solution was to create 'assembly ships' otherwise known as 'Judas goats'. The Judas goat name refers to an old herding technique where trained goats would lead sheep to a specific destination. These aircraft were modified heavy bombers such as a B-17 Flying Fortress or a B-24 Liberator. They were stripped of their armaments, given extra flares and navigational equipment and given distinctive paint schemes to make them highly visible. Bombers would line up behind the assembly ship which would peel off just before the target destination.

The DUKW

The DUKW, pronounced 'Duck', was a unique and versatile amphibious vehicle used by the Allies during World War II. Developed by the National Defense Research Committee, the unusual name came from the nomenclature used by the manufacturer, the General Motors Corporation. 'D' denotes the design year of 1942, 'U' denotes utility, 'K' denotes all wheel drive and 'W' denotes tandem rear axles, both driven. The DUKW excelled at transporting goods and troops over land and water, especially across beaches. Over 21,000 were built between 1942 and 1945. They were used extensively in the Normandy landings. The design was based on the GMC CCKW cab over engine, six wheel drive military truck with added watertight hull and propeller. One in four DUKW's were fitted with a .50–calibre Browning heavy machine gun. They were also the very first vehicles where the driver could vary the tyre pressures from inside the cab. The tyres would be pumped up for road driving, where they could reach speeds of 50mph, and deflated for driving over sand. On water, DUKW's could reach 5.5 knots (6.3mph). They could carry up to 5 tonnes of cargo or 25 fully equipped soldiers. One of the DUKW's designers, Dennis Puleston a British adventurer, sailor and environmentalist, would go on to play a key role in the banning of DDT in the USA and save the Osprey from extinction in North America.

A DUKW emerging from the sea

DUKW's were based on the GMC CCKW

King George VI touring the Normandy beaches on 16th June 1944

The Boeing B-29 Superfortress

Entering military service in 1944, the Boeing B-29 Superfortress was the result of a colossal $3 billion US design programme. It was intended for use as a long-range, high altitude bomber. Technologically advanced, it incorporated the first ever pressurised cabin in an Allied aircraft. It also had a computer-controlled firing system allowing a gunner to direct four remote machine gun turrets. With a wingspan of 141 feet, it could fly up to 328mph with a remarkable range of up to 3,250 miles carrying significant payloads. During the war, it could fly up to altitudes of 31,850 feet, avoiding nearly all enemy

The USAAF B-29 Superfortress

fighters which could not fly so high. In 1945, two B-29's (Enola Gay and Bockscar) were used to drop the nuclear bombs on Hiroshima and Nagasaki, making the B-29 the only aircraft ever to drop nuclear weapons in combat.

The V-2 Rocket

The V-2 rocket was a remarkable weapon. Travelling at great speed, it was virtually undetectable. Developed by Wernher von Braun and his team at Peenemünde, the V-2 rocket was the world's first long-range guided ballistic missile. It stood approximately 14 metres (46 feet) tall, weighed 12.5 tons, and could reach speeds of up to 5,760 kilometres per hour (3,580 miles per hour). The V-2 was powered by a liquid-fuel engine, carried a one-ton warhead and was capable of reaching altitudes of over 180 kilometres (112 miles) during its parabolic trajectory. Though developed in 1942, the V-2 did not become fully operational until 1944. By then hope of a German victory was zero, so it was used as a bargaining chip to avoid the unconditional surrender that the Allies demanded. Around 1,500 of the 'vengeance weapons' were launched against London and the South East leaving over 7,000 dead. Because of their limited range, South London was particularly hard hit and even now the effects can be seen. Evidence of their devastating consequences are noticeable if you walk through the suburb of Streatham in London where rows of Victorian houses are interrupted by buildings of post-war design. This is often a tell-tale sign that a V-2 rocket destroyed the existing houses. There are

The V-2 Rocket

plaques commemorating the dead where, such was the impact of the rocket, tragically whole families were taken at once. One of the most significant impacts of the V-2 program was its influence on post-war rocket development. After the war, many of the German scientists, including Wernher von Braun were brought to the USA and the Soviet Union as part of Operation Paperclip. They played pivotal roles in the development of both countries' space programs, including the Apollo missions.

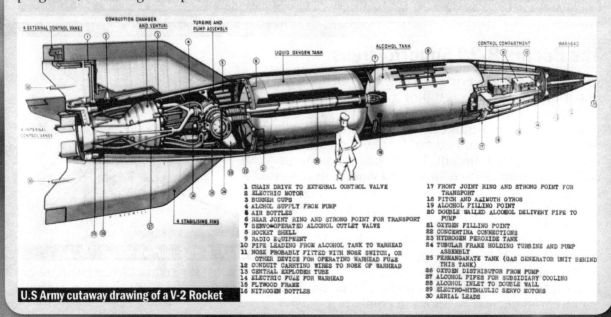

U.S Army cutaway drawing of a V-2 Rocket

1 CHAIN DRIVE TO EXTERNAL CONTROL VALVE
2 ELECTRIC MOTOR
3 BURNER CUPS
4 ALCOHOL SUPPLY FROM PUMP
5 AIR BOTTLES
6 REAR JOINT RING AND STRONG POINT FOR TRANSPORT
7 SERVO-OPERATED ALCOHOL OUTLET VALVE
8 ROCKET SHELL
9 RADIO EQUIPMENT
10 PIPE LEADING FROM ALCOHOL TANK TO WARHEAD
11 NOSE PROBABLY FITTED WITH NOSE SWITCH, OR OTHER DEVICE FOR OPERATING WARHEAD FUZE
12 CONDUIT CARRYING WIRES TO NOSE OF WARHEAD
13 CENTRAL EXPLODER TUBE
14 ELECTRIC FUZE FOR WARHEAD
15 PLYWOOD FRAME
16 NITROGEN BOTTLES

17 FRONT JOINT RING AND STRONG POINT FOR TRANSPORT
18 PITCH AND AZIMUTH GYROS
19 ALOCHOL FILLING POINT
20 DOUBLE WALLED ALCOHOL DELIVERY PIPE TO PUMP
21 OXYGEN FILLING POINT
22 CONCERTINA CONNECTIONS
23 HYDROGEN PEROXIDE TANK
24 TUBULAR FRAME HOLDING TURBINE AND PUMP ASSEMBLY
25 PERMANGANATE TANK (GAS GENERATOR UNIT BEHIND THIS TANK)
26 OXYGEN DISTRIBUTOR FROM PUMP
27 ALCOHOL PIPES FOR SUBSIDIARY COOLING
28 ALCOHOL INLET TO DOUBLE WALL
29 ELECTRO-HYDRAULIC SERVO MOTORS
30 AERIAL LEADS

The Messerschmitt Me 262

The Messerschmitt Me 262, known as the Schwalbe (Swallow) in German, was a revolutionary jet-powered fighter aircraft introduced by the German Luftwaffe in 1944. It represented a significant leap in aviation technology and was the world's first operational jet-powered fighter ahead of the British Gloster Meteor. Development of the Me 262 began in the early 1940s under the leadership of the brilliant engineer Willy Messerschmitt. The aircraft was powered by two Junkers Jumo 004

An Me 262A at the National Museum of the USAF

turbojet engines and featured swept-back wings, providing it with impressive speed and agility. It had a top speed of around 540 miles per hour and could climb at a rate of nearly 4000 feet per minute. It posed a serious threat to Allied aircraft due to its speed and advanced technology. The Me 262 was used primarily as a fighter-bomber and interceptor, attacking Allied bomber formations and inflicting significant losses. It was one of the first aircraft to be equipped with air-to-air missiles, a precursor to modern guided missiles. However, production delays, resource shortages, and Allied bombing raids hampered its deployment in large numbers. Ultimately, the Me 262 came too late to significantly alter the course of the war.

The Arado Ar 234

Germany unveiled another turbojet powered bomber in 1944. The four-engined Arado Ar 234 was a high altitude bomber and reconnaissance aircraft that could fly up to speeds of 460mph. With this kind of speed and an ability to fly over 30,000 feet, the Arado could fly beyond the reach of many Allied fighters. The Ar 234 had a bomb carrying capacity of 1,500kg making it potentially a very potent weapon.

An Me 262A at the National Museum of the USAF

However, in 1944, Germany was struggling on a number of fronts including a lack of construction materials, a lack of high quality aviation fuel and a lack of pilots. Add to this the new and untested technology of the jet engine, the history files reveal a checkered development with many prototype aircraft destroyed and test pilots killed in accidents. Due to the very long takeoff runs required, booster rockets were mounted under the wings which would jettison on takeoff. Reliability was also a big issue as the engines needed servicing every 10-25 flight hours. Overall 224 Arados were produced, with some involved in the Battle of the Bulge in December 1944. Otherwise known as the Ardennes Offensive, this was the last major offensive German campaign on the Western Front during World War II.

The D-Day landings were a long planned invasion of Mainland Europe by the Allies. Through deception and misinformation the Allies had convinced Nazi High Command that Normandy would not be the site of the landings. Thus the beaches were not as heavily defended as they might have been. The operation, code named Neptune, saw five beaches targeted: code names Omaha, Juno, Sword, Utah and Gold. Here we look at two of them:

Code Name Sword Beach | *The Normandy coast north of Caen*

The main British objective on D-Day was to seize the city of Caen. Caen is the largest city in the area and the one which all major roads in the Normandy countryside run through. On one side were the Allies: 1st Corps of General Miles Dempsey's 2nd Army, including 3rd and 6th Divisions and 4th Special Service (Commando) Brigade; 1st Commando Brigade landed 3,4,6 and 45 RM Commando, along with elements of 10 Commando. Opposing were the Axis forces: General Friedrich Dollmann's 7th Army including 21st Panzer Division under Field Marshal Erwin Rommel's personal authority. The British forces that landed at Sword Beach had multiple objectives. Some Commando Brigade units were to link up with the Juno beachhead to the west; others were to drive southwards, cutting through to the bridges

Landing on Queen sector at Sword Beach

north of Caen. These had been captured and were now being held by 6th Airborne Division. Together with Canadian forces from Juno beach, 3rd Division was to take Caen, or at least 'effectively mask' the town in the carefully chosen words of 1st Corps commander Lieutenant General John Crocker. At Sword, as at Gold and Juno, British troops faced fierce but short-lived German opposition and a friendly reception from the local population. By the end of the day, only the second of the force's main objectives was met, with the occupation of an extensive tract of territory east of the River Orne. The troops in the area were reinforced that evening by a massive drop of glider-borne infantry and equipment, protected by a Spitfire and Mustang escort. The objectives of linking up with Juno and taking Caen were precluded by opposition from German land forces, the first which the invasion force had faced. British troops on the road to Caen were first held for several hours by 21st Panzer, then forced to fall back to Bieville, three miles outside Caen. The sheer rapidity of the landing, and the congestion on the beachhead which followed, left British forces dangerously spread out and vulnerable to counter attacks from 21st Panzer, operating in the corridor between the Gold/Juno and Sword beachheads. However, by the end of the day, in spite of the main objective of the capture of the city of Caen not being achieved, the landings at Sword beach can be regarded as a success. Of the almost 29,000 troops that landed on Sword Beach, there were 683 casualties, a relatively low number as far as Normandy beach landings went.

German prisoners being marched along Sword Beach

Code Name Omaha Beach | *The Normandy coast east of Port-en-Bessin*

The largest of the D-Day assault areas, Omaha Beach, stretched over six miles between the fishing port of Port-en-Bessin to the east and the mouth of the Vire River to the west. The western third of the beach was backed by a 10ft high seawall whilst the whole beach was overlooked by cliffs 100ft high. There were five exits from the sand and shingle beach; the best was a paved road in a ravine leading to the resort village of Vierville-sur-Mer. Two were only dirt paths, and two were dirt roads leading to the villages of Belleville-sur-Mer and Saint-Laurent-sur-Mer. The Germans, under Field Marshal Erwin Rommel, had built strong defences to protect this enclosed battlefield. The waters and beach were heavily mined and there were 13 strongholds called Widerstandsneste (resistance nests). Numerous other fighting positions lined the area, supported by an extensive trench system. The defending forces consisted of three battalions of the veteran 352nd Infantry Division. Their weapons were fixed to cover the beach with flanking fire, as well as plunging fire from the cliffs. Omaha was a killing zone. It was part of the invasion area assigned to the US First Army, under Lieutenant General Omar Bradley. The beach was to be assaulted at 0630 hours by the US 1st Infantry Division, with the 116th Regiment of the 29th Division attached for D-Day

US troops climbing the bluff

only. Omaha was wide enough to land two regiments side by side with armour in front. The objectives of the 1st Division were ambitious. First it was to capture the villages of Vierville, Saint-Laurent and Colleville; then it was to push through and cut the Bayeux-Isigny road. Elements of the 16th Regiment were to link up at Port-en-Bessin with British units from Gold Beach to the east. From the beginning everything went wrong at Omaha. Specially adapted Sherman tanks, that were supposed to support the 116th Regiment, sank in the choppy waters of the Channel. Only 2 of the 29 launched made it to the beach. Only one unit of 116th landed where it was supposed to. Strong winds and tidal currents carried the landing craft from right to left. The 16th Regiment on the east half of the beach did not fare much better, landing in a state of confusion with units badly intermingled. Throughout the landing, German gunners poured deadly fire into the ranks of the invading Americans. Bodies lay on the beach or floated in the water. Men sought refuge behind beach obstacles pondering the deadly sprint across the beach to the seawall which offered the hope of safety at the base of the cliff. Destroyed craft and vehicles littered the beach and water's edge. At 0830 hours, all landing ceased at Omaha. Slowly, and in small groups, they scaled the cliffs. Meanwhile, navy destroyers steamed in scraping their hulls in the shallow water. They blasted the German fortifications at point-blank range. By 1200 hours, German fire had noticeably decreased as the defensive positions were taken from the rear. Then, one by one, the exits were opened. By nightfall, the 1st and 29th divisions held positions around Vierville, Saint-Laurent and Colleville; nowhere near the planned objectives, but they had a foothold. The Americans suffered 2,400 casualties at Omaha on June 6th, but by the end of the day they had landed 34,000 troops. The German 352nd Division lost 20 percent of its strength, with 1,200 casualties and no reserves coming to continue the fight.

This Sherman tank was abandoned after becoming bogged down in the sand

The Victoria Cross

Awarded to:
Lance Corporal Francis Arthur Jefferson

Awarded for incredible acts of bravery in the face of enemy fire at the Battle of Monte Cassino in May 1944. This is an abridged version of the Victoria Cross citation:

Lance Corporal Jefferson (centre)

"On 16th May 1944, during an attack on the Gustav Line, an anti-tank obstacle held, up some of our tanks, leaving the leading Company of Fusilier Jefferson's Battalion to dig in on the hill without tanks or anti-tank guns. The enemy counter-attacked with infantry and two Mark IV tanks, which opened fire at short range causing a number of casualties, and eliminating one P.I.A.T. (Projector, Infantry, Anti-tank) group entirely. As the tanks advanced towards the partially dug trenches, Fusilier Jefferson, entirely on his own initiative, seized a P.I.A.T. and running forward alone under heavy fire, took up a position behind a hedge; as he could not see properly, he came into the open, and standing up under a hail of bullets, fired at the leading tank which was now only twenty yards away. It burst into flames and all the crew were killed. Fusilier Jefferson then reloaded the P.I.A.T. and proceeded towards the second tank, which withdrew before he could get within range. By this time our own tanks had arrived and the enemy counter-attack was smashed with heavy casualties. Fusilier Jefferson's gallant act not merely saved the lives of his Company and caused many casualties to the Germans, but also broke up the enemy counter-attack and had a decisive effect on the subsequent operation. His supreme gallantry and disregard of personal risk contributed very largely to the success of the action."

Awarded to:
Junior Commissioned Officer (Jemadar) Abdul Hafiz

On 6th April 1944, Rao Abdul Hafiz Khan and his men were ordered to attack Japanese forces on a hill overlooking them. This is an abridged version of the Victoria Cross citation:

".. Abdul Hafiz led the attack ... up a completely bare slope with no cover, and was very steep near the crest ... On reaching the crest, Jemadar Abdul Hafiz was wounded in the leg ... So fierce was the attack, and all his men so inspired by the determination of Jemadar Abdul Hafiz to kill all enemy in sight at whatever cost, that the enemy ... ran away down the opposite slope of the hill ... Jemadar Abdul Hafiz was badly wounded in the chest from this machine-gun fire and collapsed ... attempting to fire at the retreating enemy, and shouting at the same time "Re-organise on the position and I will give covering fire." He died shortly afterwards. The inspiring leadership and great bravery displayed by Jemadar Abdul Hafiz in spite of having been twice wounded ... so encouraged his men that the

Abdul Hafiz

position was captured ... The complete disregard for his own safety and his determination to capture and hold the position at all costs was an example to all ranks, which it would be difficult to equal." At just 18-years old Abdul Hafiz became the youngest VC recipient from the British Indian Army. He is buried in Imphal Indian War Cemetery. His VC is on display in the Lord Ashcroft Gallery at the Imperial War Museum, London.

Medal of Freedom (USA) and Légion d'honneur (France)

Awarded to: **Marlene Dietrich**

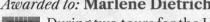

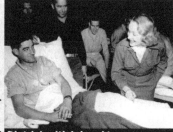

During two tours for the United Service Organization Inc. in 1944 and 1945 Dietrich, who was born in Germany, but was a fervent anti-Nazi, performed for Allied troops in Algeria, Britain, Italy, France and the Netherlands. She then entered Germany with General George Patton's Brigade. When asked why she had done this, in spite of the obvious danger of being within a few miles of German lines, she replied "aus Anstand" (translation: out of decency). It was remarked at the time that she was at the front lines more often than the Supreme Commander Dwight D. Eisenhower. As part of her show, she would claim to have been taught mind-reading by Orson Welles. Dietrich would inform the audience that she could read minds and ask them to concentrate on whatever came into their heads. Then she would walk over to a soldier and earnestly tell him "Oh, think of something else. I can't possibly talk about that!" In 1944, the Morale Operations Branch of the Office of Strategic Services (OSS) initiated the Musak project which broadcast musical propaganda designed to demoralise enemy soldiers. Dietrich, the only performer who was made aware that her recordings would be used by the OSS, recorded a number of songs for the project, including *Lili Marleen*, a favourite of soldiers on both sides of the conflict. Major General William J. Donovan, head of the OSS, wrote to Dietrich "I am personally deeply grateful for your generosity in making these recordings for us."

USA

France

Dietrich with injured troops

The Order of Victory (USSR)

The Order of Victory is the most distinguished of all orders ever awarded to anyone in Russia. It is also one of the rarest in the world; only 22 copies were made. The medal is thought to be the most expensive honour in the world. If it could theoretically be posted at any auction, the starting price would be more than £15 million. The last recipient of the medal, Michael I of Romania, died in 2017. However, the fate of his medallion is unclear. Officially, it is stored in Michael I's estate in Versoix, Canton of Geneva, Switzerland. But there are rumours Michael I sold his Order in the 1980s for about £3million. The Order of Victory was awarded only to Generals and Marshals for their actions in planning and military

Marshal Georgy Zhukov (centre)

administration resulting in a "successful operation within the framework of one or several fronts resulting in a radical change of the situation in favour of the Red Army." Each Order of Victory is made of platinum, while the inscription 'ПОБЕДА' ("Victory") is made out of gold. The medallion has 174 diamonds (16 karats in total) and 5 artificial 5-karat rubies, 25 karats in each. The Order was first awarded was on the 10th April 1944 to Marshal Georgy Zhukov, Marshal Alexander Vasilevsky and the Commander-in-Chief Joseph Stalin. All three were awarded in honour of the liberation of the right-bank of the Dnieper River. In 1945, the same three commanders were honoured with the Order for the second time.

The Tragic Death of Guy Gibson

Guy Gibson was one of Bomber Command's most famous officers. He was awarded the Victoria Cross for his bravery and leadership during the legendary Dambuster Raid of 1943. As other Lancaster bombers from 617 Squadron approached their target, Gibson flew his Lancaster alongside them to effectively double-up the amount of fire from the aircraft that could be aimed at German gun emplacements on top of their targeted dam. Gibson was seen as too valuable in terms of his propaganda value to be allowed to fly after the raid. He toured America and Britain and was effectively retired from engaging the enemy by his superiors. However, after a great deal of pleading, Gibson was allowed to fly 'in anger' once more. While returning from one of his subsequent missions over Europe, his Mosquito crashed. Gibson and his navigator, Jim Warwick, were tragically died on 19th September 1944. The official cause of the crash has always attracted a degree of scepticism among

Wing Commander Guy Gibson

aviation historians. As no one could officially say what happened, two theories were put forward. The first was that Gibson ran out of fuel and crashed as a result. Critics of this hypothesis countered it with their belief that Gibson was too skilled a pilot to allow something so basic to bring him down. It was also said that if Gibson could fly a Lancaster bomber at such low heights as the Dambuster Raid required, he was certainly skilled enough to glide down a Mosquito to enable a decent crash landing even if he had run out of fuel. The second theory was that Gibson was flying his Mosquito very low, which he was certainly skilled enough to do, but was hit by

Gibson (on the ladder) and his crew boarding for Operation Chastise: The Dambusters raid

enemy ground fire. However, in October 2011 a new cause was put forward to explain Gibson's death. Newly found evidence indicated very clearly that Gibson's Mosquito was brought down by what is now termed 'friendly fire'. A British bomber returning from a night time raid over Nazi Germany mistook the low-flying Mosquito for a Luftwaffe aircraft and shot at it accordingly. Sergeant Bernard McCormack, a gunner in a Lancaster bomber, believed that he mistook Gibson's Mosquito for a Junkers-88. Many bombers got lost or flew off course on the return leg of their flight to their British bases. Added to this, crew members would have been on high alert and possibly 'trigger happy' due to the very real threat of being attacked. Once McCormack became convinced that he had shot down Gibson's Mosquito, he remained quiet. He died in 1992, but not before he recorded onto tape what he believed had happened. Official RAF reports on the crash stated that no other aircraft was in the vicinity of Gibson's Mosquito when he crashed, hence the running out of fuel and being shot from the ground theories prevailing. However, the flight combat report of Sergeant Bernard McCormack's Lancaster clearly shows that he was in the vicinity where Guy Gibson would have been flying.

The Lost Battalion

In October 1944, the 36th Infantry Division (a Texas National Guard unit) was fighting in the Vosges Mountains in south-eastern France close to the German border. The 36th had been through a rough war in Italy, being almost overrun by German panzers at the Salerno landings. The Division was also nearly decimated whilst crossing the Rapido River in January 1944, before it was transferred to southern France. By late 1944, it was battling its way through the cold, forested mountains that barred the path into Germany. Misfortune struck again. A badly planned attack sent the 36th Division's 141st Regiment four miles

1st Battalion members after their rescue

deep into German lines. This was despite fears that the Germans, masters of the swift counter-attack, would cut them off. The Germans did indeed counter-attack, trapping the 1st Battalion. According to one account: "The Lost Battalion's situation was desperate. Isolated for six days, the Texans had beaten back five enemy assaults. Deaths and casualties mounted, yet they couldn't evacuate the bodies. They pooled their meagre supplies of food and ammunition and risked German sniper fire to get water. The Allies tried to send supplies. First they shot shells filled with chocolate, but the shelling caused casualties. A few days later the Allies dropped supplies by parachute, but most of the packages landed in German-occupied positions." But relief came, in the form of the 442nd Regimental Combat Team, the most decorated unit in the history of the US Army winning more than 18,000 decorations. It also happened to be an all-Nisei (Japanese-American) outfit, one of only three such units in the US Army. It was composed of volunteers and draftees from Hawaii and mainland United States, many of whose families were languishing in camps while the sons fought and died on the battlefield. Despite racism in an army already segregated into white and black units, the 442nd, whose motto was "Go for Broke", had already earned an enviable reputation in Italy before being attached to the 36th Division in France. Through heavy rain in the muddy, wooded hills that deprived the Americans of tank and air support, the 442nd fought for six days to reach the Texans. Casualties were so heavy that clerks and cooks became riflemen. With a steep drop on the left and right, the men had no choice but to go straight up the middle. Private Barney Hajiro was pinned down on the ridge. He saw enemy machine guns kill eight and wound 21 of his comrades. Then suddenly, a few men, including Hajiro decided to 'go for broke.' He charged up the ridge, shooting his Browning automatic rifle and running 100 yards under fire. He single-handedly destroyed two machine

gun nests and took out two enemy snipers. His brave actions spurred his comrades to rally and boldly attack. Hajiro was awarded a Medal of Honour. The Japanese-Americans of the 442nd rescued 211 survivors of the Lost Battalion. The price they paid was 800 Nisei casualties. When Division Commander Dahlquist ordered the 442nd to assemble for a recognition ceremony, he scolded a 442nd colonel: "You disobeyed my orders. I told you to present the whole regiment." The colonel looked him in the eye and reportedly said: "General, this is the regiment. The rest are either dead or in the hospital."

In 2009, veterans attended the 65th anniversary tribute

Noor Inayat Khan

Having grown up in Britain and France and a descendant of Indian royalty, bilingual Noor Inayat Khan was recruited by the elite Special Operations Executive (SOE) in 1942 to work in Paris as a radio operator. Records from the national archives show that she was the first female wireless operator sent to Nazi-occupied France during World War II. Brave, glamorous and formidable, it is said she acted not out of a love for Britain, but out of a loathing of fascism and dictatorial rule. Noor was raised with strong principles, believing in religious tolerance and non-violence. Her great-great-great-grandfather was Tipu Sultan, an 18th century Muslim ruler of Mysore. He refused to submit to British rule and was killed in battle in 1799. Born on 1st January 1914 in Russia to an Indian father and American mother, the agent's infancy was spent in London. Her father was a musician and Sufi teacher. The family moved to France when she was a child and lived in Paris, where she was educated and learnt fluent French. The national archives describe how the sensitive

Noor Inayat Khan

young woman studied both medicine and music. In 1939, the Twenty Jataka Tales, a collection of traditional Indian children's stories, she had retold was published in Le Figaro. When war broke out in 1939, she trained up as a nurse with the French Red Cross. She fled the country just before the government surrendered to Germany in November 1940, escaping by boat to England with her mother and sister. Shortly after arriving in the UK, she joined the Women's Auxiliary Air Force (WAAF) as a wireless operator, soon catching the attention of recruiters from the Special Operations Executive. Code named 'Madeleine', she joined others in the 'Prosper' resistance network in Paris. This was led Francis Suttill, code named 'Prosper'. He was famously tasked by Prime Minister Winston Churchill to "set

A B2 portable radio transceiver as used by Noor and other continental resistance spies to communicate with the SOE in London

Europe ablaze". Noor sent valuable information back to England. Despite suspicions that the network had been infiltrated by a Nazi spy, Khan refused to return to Britain, risking arrest. With her team gradually captured by the Gestapo, Noor continued for as long as possible to send intercepted radio messages back to England. Despite her commanders urging her to return, she single-handedly ran a cell of spies across Paris for three more months, frequently changing her appearance and aliases. Eventually, she was betrayed, arrested and imprisoned. She was sent to Pforzheim prison in Germany where she was kept shackled in solitary confinement. She was then transferred to Dachau concentration camp where she was tortured and eventually shot by the German Gestapo on the 13th September 1944. Her final word, uttered as the German firing squad raised their weapons, was simply: "Liberté". For her bravery, she was posthumously awarded the George Cross. In France, she was honoured with the Croix de Guerre and later with two memorials and an annual ceremony marking her death.

Juan Pujol García

This story reads like something out of a John le Carré novel, and in many ways he was the perfect spy. After the war, an MI5 spy named Juan Pujol García faked his own death and kept it secret for almost four decades. But that is not even the most interesting thing about him. Pujol was a veteran of the Spanish Civil War who had come to loathe totalitarianism, both in Francisco Franco and Adolf Hitler. Upon the outbreak of war in 1939, he was determined to join the British war effort as a spy against Germany. He was so determined that he wasn't deterred when British officers turned him down as he didn't have any connections or credentials. Instead, he formulated a plan to pad his C.V. while aiding the war effort. Posing as a Spanish official who was

Juan Pujol García

flying to London, Pujol made contact with Nazi officials in Madrid and told them that he was interested in spying on Britain for the Third Reich. He began sending the Nazis false information that they thought was from London, but which was actually fed from Lisbon and Madrid. Essentially, Pujol became a rogue double agent whom Britain didn't even know it had. Though Pujol sent Germany false reports, he used lots of factual information to make them appear legitimate. In 1942, he again approached British officials about becoming a double agent by showing them that, in fact, he already was one. Unbeknown to him, British operatives had already realised that a secret spy was sending information to Germany, but didn't know who that spy was. When Pujol revealed himself, they brought him to London to work for MI5. The Nazis continued to view Pujol as an important spy throughout the war. They never discovered that he was a double agent, despite the fact that a lot of his information was incorrect. Pujol's MI5 codename was Agent Garbo because he was such a good actor. The Germans also felt that if they cut him off or if they doubted him even, they were not going to just lose one agent, they were going lose a network of 27 spies. In his most famous deception, Pujol told the Nazis that news they had heard about a planned invasion of Normandy was fake. Of course, this wasn't true, and as a result the Nazis were unprepared for the Allies' successful D-Day invasion. He also told the Nazis that their V-1 and V-2 rockets were

Tomás Harris, Pujol's case officer at MI5

overshooting London, leading to the German military adjusting their trajectory, thus saving many lives. After the European war ended in 1945, Pujol continued to work for MI5 to investigate whether Germany had any plans to resurrect a sort of Fourth Reich. After this, Pujol wanted to get out of Europe and away from his memories of the war, so he moved to Venezuela. But, because many former Nazis had also chosen Venezuela as a place to flee from their crimes, he figured it would be safer for him there if everybody thought he was dead.

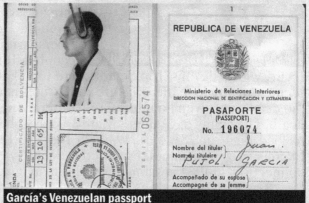

García's Venezuelan passport

Slapton Sands

Exercise Tiger was one of a number of large scale rehearsals for the D-Day landings in Normandy. It was a disaster on an epic scale. Late in 1943, the British government designated the beach at Slapton Sands in Devon a training ground due to its similarity to the Utah beach in Normandy that US troops would invade on D-Day. So vital was the exercise that the commanders ordered the use of live naval and artillery ammunition to make the exercise as realistic as possible. This was to accustom the soldiers to what they were soon going to experience. The first tragedy occurred on the 27th April 1944 when a late change to the H-Hour (Zero Hour) for the practice assault resulted in a so-called 'friendly fire' incident with an unknown number of casualties. Rumour suggests that over 400 men were killed. The second tragedy occurred early the next day when eight tank landing ships

US troops landing on Slapton Sands during D-Day rehearsals

full of US troops converged in nearby Lyme Bay, making their way towards Slapton Sands for the rehearsal. Unbeknown to them, a group of German high-speed Schnellboote (code named E-Boats by the allies) had been alerted by heavy radio traffic in the Lyme Bay area. They intercepted the three-mile long convoy of vessels. To make matters worse, a British Navy destroyer which should have been escorting the convoy at the rear had been earlier ordered into Plymouth for repairs. Its replacement was still en route. The heavily-laden, slow-moving tank landing ships were easy targets for the torpedo boats. They first attacked the unprotected rear of the convoy. Three of the tank landing ships were hit by German torpedoes and two quickly sunk. More loss of life was caused by life jackets being worn incorrectly around waists under backpacks with soldiers drowning or dying of hypothermia. The exercise that killed nearly 1,000 American servicemen was considered by US top brass

The Sherman Tank at Torcross Memorial

to be such a disaster that they ordered a complete information blackout. Any survivor who revealed the truth about what happened would be threatened with a court-martial. The Allied commanders were also concerned officers who went missing during the attack could have ended up in German hands, where they might reveal the Allied intentions for the D-Day landings. The commanders even considered changing details of the operation. However, the bodies of every one of those officers with 'BIGOT' (British Invasion of German Occupied Territory) level clearance, a code name for a security level beyond Top Secret, were found and the tactics of D-Day were deemed to be secure. An article in the US Stars and Stripes magazine after the war said family members of the dead were given no information other than what was in the original message about their death. The family of Gunner's Mate 3rd Class Thanuel Shappard only knew the bare facts that he had died on 28th April 1944. In the late 1980s, while watching a documentary about Exercise Tiger, his mother noticed the date was the same as her son's death and made the connection. In 1984, a submerged Sherman tank was raised from the seabed and restored. It stands on Slapton Sands as a memorial and unofficial tombstone for the hundreds who died on those tragic days, many of whom are buried in unmarked graves.

Operation Valkyrie

In all, Adolph Hitler survived 23 known attempts on his life. The July 20th Plot, or Operation Valkyrie, was the closest any of the would-be assassins got to achieving their aims. When the operation was first conceived, it had nothing to do with assassination attempts or coups. Rather it was created because the German government was concerned that allied bombing of its cities would lead to civil unrest. Consequently, they created a plan to see if the Territorial Army could take control and maintain civil government in the event of civil breakdown. Several generals, who were enthusiastic supporters of Hitler when the war was going well, were now tired of their Führer's increasingly erratic behaviour. They also thought that with Hitler out of the way, they could sue for a peace short of the unconditional surrender demanded by the Allies. The plan was that General Stauffenberg would detonate a bomb during Hitler's round table meeting at the Wolfsschanze (the Wolf's lair). With Hitler dead, the conspirators would claim that Nazi insiders set off the bomb. They would arrest the SS and establish a new government with Friedrich Goerdeler, an anti-Nazi as Chancellor. On 20th July 1944, Claus von Stauffenberg arrived at Hitler's military conference at the Wolfsschanze. The bomb was concealed in his briefcase. Due to the hot weather, the

Martin Bormann, Hermann Göring, and Bruno Loerzer inspect the damaged conference room

conference location was changed from the underground bunker to the main meeting room. After planting the briefcase bomb, Stauffenberg took a pre-arranged phone call and left the Wolfsschanze. Whilst leaving the compound, another officer unwittingly moved Stauffenberg's briefcase, propping it against a thick oak table leg. At approximately 12:45 PM, the bomb exploded, killing three officers and destroying the room. However, Hitler was shielded by the solid wooden table leg and survived with nothing but a perforated eardrum and cuts and bruises. Meanwhile, Stauffenberg travelled to a nearby airfield and flew three hours to Berlin. Whilst travelling, however, his fellow conspirators failed to act. They were unsure whether Hitler was, in fact, dead or not. By the time Stauffenberg landed in Berlin, it was already too late. Although Hitler had survived, the conspirators managed to disarm the SS and Nazi Intelligence. However, Heinrich Himmler, the SS Reichsfuhrer regained control. Previously enthusiastic conspirators began to change sides. Retribution was swift and brutal. Of the around 200 conspirators, 180 were rounded up, tortured and executed. Even though the plot failed, it had a marked effect on how the last year of the war would play out. The Nazis had lost most of their leading generals, including Erwin Rommel, who chose to take his own life rather than be questioned about any involvement in the coup attempt. This greatly reduced the Wehrmacht's ability to defend or even counter-attack. It also left Himmler in a more powerful position as he took over control as commander of the defence branch of the German Army from Friedrich Fromm, who was executed for his role in the plot.

Hitler's tattered trousers

George Orwell once said that sport was "war minus the shooting", but in 1944 war made sport almost irrelevant. Sport in Britain had virtually shut down, and that which was played was mainly to boost morale. There was no Wimbledon Tennis Championship, the centre court had even taken a direct hit in 1940. The French Open Tennis tournament was the only one of the 'Big Four' to take place. However, as the championship was played under Nazi control, the results were voided after the war. Official football, rugby and cricket leagues were suspended. Horse racing continued, but only in areas away from our major towns and cities. Wartime leagues were set up in both rugby and association football. Sportsmen and sportswomen had signed up for the services. When they returned on leave, many would turn

George Orwell

out for a team they were stationed near. It gave a lot of people the chance to see their idols in the flesh for the first time. Women's football thrived as factory teams were set up, though no official leagues were formed. The Olympics that were due to be held in London did take place, but only in a prisoner of war camp. Polish prisoners at the Woldenberg camp were granted permission by their German captors to stage an unofficial 'POW Olympics' between 23rd July and 13th August 1944. An Olympic flag, made with a bed sheet and pieces of coloured fabric, was raised. The event is widely

A women's football match on a snow covered pitch in Fallowfield

considered to be a demonstration of how the Olympic spirit can transcend war. London would go on to stage the postponed games in 1948; Germany and Japan were not invited. Many sports women and men lost the best years of their lives, or worse still lost their lives during the war. One of the greatest sportsmen ever, cricketer Don Bradman, joined the Australian army and suffered an injury in training. Medical examination showed that he had poor eyesight, remarkable for a man who averaged nearly a hundred with the bat. The war impinged on sport in many different ways: Leigh rugby league team had to abandon their ground when a neighbouring cable factory needed to expand. Even in countries untouched directly by the ravages of war, sport was seen as an unnecessary distraction. Though the American mainland was not directly threatened, many sports were seen as frivolous in a time of great national crisis. Sports stars either enlisted or turned their efforts to fundraising for the war.

Don Bradman

When we think of London in wartime, we think of air raid shelters, food rations and the Blitz spirit in the face of death from above. What is less well known is that people were so determined to carry on as normal that they would risk their lives to watch and play football in stadiums that were obvious targets for the Luftwaffe. Football became a key component of the morale that would keep Britain going in times of terrifying adversity. The 1939-40 season was only three games old when it was abandoned, after Neville Chamberlain announced the country was at war with Germany. Everton were reigning champions and Portsmouth the cup holders. The Football League couldn't continue after the government banned the assembly of crowds. Hundreds of professional footballers joined the Armed Forces, though many joined the reserve

A flying header beats the goalkeeper

police or Territorial Army. This kept them in the UK available for either football or war, whichever was the most pressing. It wasn't long though before appeals to reopen the football grounds were heard. Factory workers wanted to enjoy their Saturday afternoons off. With travel severely restricted, the joint FA-League War Emergency Committee allowed regional competitions to take place; wartime leagues and the Football League War Cup were established. Mass Observation, the UK's social research organisation declared: "Sports like football have an absolute effect on the morale of the people and one Saturday afternoon of league matches could probably do more to affect people's

A British Army team playing in Rome in 1944

spirits than the recent Government poster campaign urging cheerfulness." Arsenal's Highbury ground was given up to the ARP (Air Raid Precautions), so the club had to play their home games at White Hart Lane, Tottenham. This returned the favour from the first world war, when Spurs played at Arsenal. Several grounds were hit by German bombs, including The Den and The Valley. The wartime league games lacked a competitive edge, with matches played with the air of a friendly. Guests from other clubs would also play if they were stationed nearby. Consequently, the crowds for these games were small. But the Cup was different. Players and fans succumbed to the magic of it. By 1944, the Allies were growing in confidence, having taken North Africa. However, London was about to be on the end of deadly V-1 and V-2 flying bomb attacks. The largest wartime club match crowd so far was attracted to the War Cup South final between Charlton and Chelsea at Wembley where 85,000 watched Charlton win 3-1. The guest of honour was the commanding officer of the American forces in Europe, General Eisenhower. He told reporters "I started cheering for the Blues, but when I saw the Reds were winning, well I had to start cheering for them." Charlton met Aston Villa in the national final on 20th May 1944, drawing 1-1 at Stamford Bridge in front of 38,540. However, due to renewed bombing threats, a replay was ruled out. The cup was shared. All in all, some 37 million watched football during the six years of the second world war, showing a side to the Blitz spirit that's rarely remarked on.

There was little meaningful Rugby Union in 1944, save for a few inter-service games. A Northern Rugby League Emergency League was set up, but the call-up of so many players meant that each club played a different number of games. After finishing top, Wakefield Trinity lost to Dewsbury in the Championship play-off semi final, who in turn lost to Wigan in the final. So many players' careers were interrupted or ended by the war; no story was more remarkable than that of 'Paddy' Mayne:

Robert Blair 'Paddy' Mayne

One of seven siblings, Robert Blair 'Paddy' Mayne was born into a prosperous family in Newtownards in Northern Ireland. He was a superb athlete and all-round sportsman, most notably representing both Ireland and the British Lions at rugby. Mayne was a complex and enigmatic character. A man of great intelligence, he trained in law and had a love of literature. Yet he was also troubled and tempestuous. Overly fond of alcohol and with an outrageous sense of humour, Mayne's raucous behaviour could often spill over into violence. His behaviour during the British Lions tour of South Africa in 1938 has become the stuff of legend. Accounts of his behaviour there include smashing up hotel rooms, drunken brawling with dock workers, freeing a convict he had befriended and dumping the bloody carcass of an antelope on the floor of his hotel room following a midnight hunting adventure. Early in the war, Mayne joined the Royal Ulster Rifles. His thirst for adventure soon led him to volunteer for the Commandos, Britain's new amphibious assault troops. He served with 11 (Scottish) Commando in North Africa, before being recruited into the SAS from a prison cell, where he was awaiting court martial for striking his commanding officer. Following its disastrous opening operation in North Africa, it was Mayne who first brought badly needed success to the SAS. On the night of 14th December 1941, he led a small group attack on Tamet airfield in Libya. Mayne's team burst into the officers' mess and gunned down the Germans and Italians inside. They then set about attaching Lewes Bombs (a type of blast incendiary) to some aircraft and shooting up the cockpits of others. In total, 24 aircraft were destroyed together with fuel tanks, an ammunition dump and a line of telegraph poles. This attack is also famous for Mayne's Herculean act of wrenching out the control panel of an enemy aircraft, which has gone down in SAS legend. After the capture of David Sterling in January 1943, command of 1st SAS Regiment passed to Mayne. He rose to the challenge, leading it through campaigns in Sicily, Italy, France and Germany. In 1944, the unit took part in the Allied invasion of Northern Europe. Between June and September 1944, it operated in a guerrilla role, working behind enemy lines with French resistance fighters, to sabotage transport and industrial infrastructure, ambush enemy columns and co-ordinate air strikes. For his action in Germany, Mayne was recommended for the Victoria Cross, the highest military award for gallantry. This was later downgraded to a Distinguished Service Order (DSO). However, when added to the three other DSOs he had won in Africa, Sicily and France, this made Mayne one of the most highly decorated soldiers of the war. Injury meant that he never wore a rugby shirt in anger again.

Paddy Mayne in Egypt

That Wisden, the cricket lovers' bible, should appear in 1944 was a triumph of hope over experience. There was little to report. The County Championship in Britain was suspended and there was no Sheffield Shield in Australia. This most British of sports was put on hold except for a few Army vs Navy games at the home of cricket, Lords. London's other main venue, The Oval, had been converted into a prisoner-of-war camp, though it was never used as such. In 1939, there was a planned England tour of India which had been abandoned at the outbreak of war. The fact that many of the cricketers were good team players served them well during the war. Here is a selection of the squad, highlighting their war records. Tragically one was to die and others missed their chance of ever playing for England.

A.J. Holmes   *Right handed batsman for Sussex*

Flight Lieutenant in the RAF.

H.T. Bartlett *Left handed batsman for Sussex*

Joined the Royal Kent Regiment and served at the Normandy landings.

H. Gimblett   *Right handed batsman for Somerset*

Joined the Fire Service and helped to put out fires in the badly bombed ports of Plymouth and Bristol.

R.H. Human *Right handed batsman for Worcestershire*

Human was to go to India, not as a cricketer, but as a soldier with the Ox and Bucks Light Infantry. He died there on active service in November 1942, aged just 33.

Robert 'Bob' Wyatt

R.E.S. Wyatt *Right handed batsman for Warwickshire*

Served with distinction in the RAF.

S.C. Griffith *Right handed batsman for Sussex*

Served as second-in-command of the 6th Airborne Division for which he won the Distinguished Flying Cross.

T.P.B. Smith *Spin bowler for Essex*

Served as a staff sergeant with the Essex Regiment in Alexandria, Egypt.

Harold Gimblett

With so many men from the Empire stationed in Britain, there was ample scope for friendly cricket matches. Very often these were friendly in name only and were fiercely competitive. A drawn one-day match at Lord's between an England XI and a West Indies XI featured the young Alec Bedser and Trevor Bailey. Bedser made his mark by taking 6/27 in the West Indies first innings. In the drawn Sir PF Warner's XI v Royal Australian Air Force match at Lord's, Keith Miller top-scored in the RAAF's first innings, with 45 out of 100, as well as taking 2/20. A strong England XI beat The Dominions by 8 runs in a two-day match at Lord's. Les Ames made 133 in the England first innings whilst Denis Compton then took 6/15 in eight overs. In their second innings, The Dominions came close to snatching an unlikely victory, with Stewie Dempster making 113.

The Controversy Over Horse Racing During Wartime

With the fall of France in 1940, the ongoing debate which raged around wartime racing came to a head with an attempt to suspend all horse racing. This was avoided only when some influential members of the government argued that the recreational and morale-building benefits of the sport outweighed the negatives. The detractors on the other hand saw racing as a wasteful luxury and a drain on scarce resources in terms of transport, feed and manpower. There were constant attempts to stop or reduce it. The movement against racing was championed by Philip Noel-Baker, himself a fine sportsman who had won an Olympic 1,500 metres silver medal. Noel-Baker was a high-minded intellectual with no time for horse racing. Unfortunately for the sport, he was also Parliamentary Secretary to the Department of War Transport. When it came to fuel, he preached a message of utmost economy and transporting horses around the country came pretty near the top of his list of targets. The Home Office and the Jockey Club went head-to-head throughout the war. There was

Horse racing in wartime drew fierce opinions

constant and unseen political infighting which led to the initial suspension and then reinstatement of racing in 1940. This was followed by ever-tightening restrictions on events, number and location of courses in 1941/2 and even more minimal racing programmes in the later years of the war. Programmes were restricted to local meetings where travel requirements were minimal. This not only affected horse racing but also the very popular sport of greyhound racing which was cut to one or two meetings a week. The British betting public were seeing less and less opportunity for a flutter in a time when people were consumed by a determined effort to enjoy their lives as much as they possibly could. After all, who really knew how long it would last? A day at the wartime races was a very different, and in many ways, more exciting racing experience. It could include a bombing raid, as it once did at Newmarket. Alternatively there could be a riot of bitter anti-racing campaigners as it did on occasion at Cheltenham. There might even be an unlicensed meeting, with the murky world of illegal racing raising its ugly black-market head. Horse racing in neutral Ireland continued unaffected by the war, providing a regular and available betting market. Illicit gaming houses masqueraded as clubs with illegal betting springing up everywhere. Many of these establishments, which could be found in most of Britain's cities, were run by gangsters. Scores of these were raided by police in 1944.

The New Derby Stakes

In the Wartime Derby, held at Newmarket on 17th June 1944, trainer Jack Jarvis' top jockey Eph Smith chose the wrong horse in Tehran, leaving Billy Nevett, at home on leave from the Royal Army Ordinance Corps, to ride his second string Ocean Swell. Things certainly turned out swell for Nevett as his mount stayed on well to beat Tehran by a neck at odds of 28 to 1.

Ocean Swell

Overview

Outside of a few college events in the USA and some non-recognised events in Nazi-controlled Europe, athletics virtually ground to a halt. The 1944 Summer Olympics had been scheduled to take place in London but were cancelled, as were the 1944 Winter Olympics. Ultimately, London would host the summer games in 1948. Below, we spotlight the lives of three athletes whose careers were affected by the war.

Louis Zamperini | American distance runner

Zamperini ran in the 1936 Berlin Olympics and was training to take part in the 1940 Tokyo games, which were cancelled when war broke out. Zamperini enlisted and joined the US Army Air Corps as a bombardier. His plane was shot down near Japan. After 47 days drifting at sea on a raft, he and his fellow crew members were taken prisoner of war. They were subjected to horrendous treatment by their Japanese captors. By the time of his release at the end of the war, Zamperini's athletics career was over. He took to hard drinking, but found religion and so began a healing process. Some of his torturers received forgiveness in person in 1950, when he visited them in prison in Tokyo. In 1998, Zamperini returned to Japan once again to carry the torch at the Nagano Winter Games.

Louis Zamperini

Foy Draper | American Olympic champion sprinter

Foy Draper was an American athlete who won a gold medal in 4 × 100m Relay alongside the great Jesse Owens at the Berlin Olympics of 1936. He also reportedly held the world record for the 100-yard dash in a time of 9.4 seconds. This was all the more remarkable as he stood only 5'5" tall. During World War II, he served as a pilot in a twin-engine attack bomber A-208B 'Havoc' in North Africa. Draper took off to take part in the battle of Kassarine Pass, Tunisia. He and his two crewmen never returned and they were officially declared dead on 1st February. His body was eventually recovered. He is buried in the North African Cemetery and Memorial in Tunisia. His gravestone shows 4th January 1943 as the date of death.

William Roberts | English sprinter

William 'Bill' Roberts was an English sprinter who won a gold medal in the 4x400m relay event at the 1936 Summer Olympics in Berlin. He had further success in 1938 in the 440yd event at the British Empire games in Sydney, Australia. In Britain, many athletes were enlisted to impart their knowledge of physical training to the armed forces whilst others saw active service. When war broke out, Bill joined the RAF, in which he served with distinction. After the war he was able to resume his athletics career and captained the British team at the 1948 Olympic games in London.

Beau Jack vs Bob Montgomery | The $36 Million War Bonds Fight

4th August 1944 in New York

Beau Jack

To say that Beau Jack grew up the hard way is an understatement. Beau was born Sidney Walker, in Waynesboro, Georgia. After the death of his mother, he moved to Augusta to stay with his grandmother who affectionately called him 'Beau Jack'. He was raised during the Great Depression on a run down farm where he worked the fields. A few days a week he would rise early, walk three miles into town and shine shoes until dusk. To make extra money, he would engage in battle royales. These consisted of five to ten boys, usually black, fighting each other, often blindfolded, until only one remained standing. The winner was given a purse by the white organisers who would gamble large amounts on these unsavoury events. This is where Beau honed his boxing skills. These early encounters turned him in to one of the greatest fighters of his generation. Following a battle royale at the Augusta National Golf Club, Beau was offered a position of caddy where he met Bobby Jones who helped fund his boxing career. Some consider a bout with Montgomery on 4th August 1944 the most famous fight of Jack's career. Staged at a critical time in the Second World War, it became known as the 'War Bonds Fight' with tickets only available to purchasers of War Bonds. A ringside seat required a purchase of a $100,000 war bond. Montgomery had previously defeated Jack a year earlier, taking the World lightweight title. Although Montgomery's title was not on the line, the gate was a record $36 million with 15,822 war bonds being sold. Many people who purchased bonds charitably left their tickets at the box office to be used by American servicemen. Montgomery and Jack, who were both serving as privates in the army, refused to take purses for the fight. Jack took the fight on points after 10 rounds. However, the highlight of the evening was when the lights dimmed and a spotlight shone on Joe Louis who was standing in the front row. Soon the crowd were on their feet as Louis received a rapturous standing ovation. Beau retired with a record of 83 wins, 40 knockouts, 24 losses and 5 draws. After retirement, he ran a drive-in barbecue stand and operated a small farm in Atlanta. He refereed wrestling

Bob Montgomery

matches in South Carolina during this time. With his modest boxing earnings, he moved to Miami and returned to shoe shining, working at Miami Beach's Fontainebleau Hotel. He also trained fighters in Miami's Fifth Street Gym. Jack was inducted into the Georgia Sports Hall of Fame in 1979, and the International Boxing Hall of Fame in 1991.

The US PGA Championship

During the war golf was seen as an unnecessary diversion even in America, who by 1944 were under no threat of enemy invasion or bombardment. The home of The Masters, The Augusta National Golf Club, was turned into a farm. This had mixed results. The turkey operation was a success, but the cattle herd laid waste to the azaleas and camellias and stripped the bark from young trees. However the PGA decided that it was appropriate to hold the 1944 event, which had been cancelled in 1943. The reigning champion from 1942, Sam Snead, was laid up in a military hospital and received a discharge from the US Navy a month after the tournament. The tournament was held as matchplay. American Bob Hamilton won the final against fellow American Byron Nelson on the final hole. Nelson received some consolation when he won the medal for fewest strokes for the week. Though it was Hamilton's only major, that was not the most remarkable thing about his golfing life. In 1975, Hamilton achieved the Holy Grail

US PGA winner Bob Hamilton

for many golfers both amateur and professional; to shoot his age. Though rare, what made his achievement even more remarkable is that he scored 59 aged 59. It is a record that still stands today. One of the greatest golfers of the age, Bobby Jones, in spite of being exempt from service on account of being 40 years old, signed up and went out with the invasion force in the June 1944 D-Day Landings. General Dwight D. Eisenhower, who commanded the invasion force, would later go on to become a member at the Augusta club.

Richmond Golf Club's Temporary Wartime Rules

Early in the war, bombs dropped on Richmond Golf Club. This led the members to create a set of tongue-in-cheek wartime rules in defiance of Nazi aggression. They became world famous and even led to Hitler's Minister of Propaganda to mention them in a broadcast.

1. Players are asked to collect the bomb and shrapnel splinters to save these causing damage to the mowing machines.

2. In competition, during gunfire or while bombs are falling, players may take shelter without penalty or ceasing play.

3. The positions of known delayed action bombs are marked by red flags at a reasonable, but not guaranteed, safe distance therefrom.

4. Shrapnel and/or bomb splinters on the fairways or in bunkers within a club's length of a ball may be moved without penalty, and no penalty shall be incurred if a ball is thereby caused to move accidentally.

5. A ball moved by enemy action may be replaced or, if lost or destroyed, a ball may be dropped not nearer the hole without penalty.

6. A ball lying in a crater may be lifted and dropped not nearer the hole, preserving the line to the hole, without penalty.

7. A player whose stroke is affected by the simultaneous explosion of a bomb may play another ball. Penalty one stroke.

LEND TO DEFEND HIS RIGHT TO BE FREE

BUY NATIONAL SAVINGS CERTIFICATES

Photo Credits

Credits shown in the order in which they appear in the book. Photos not listed are in the public domain.

Key to page numbers

fc = front cover; **ifc** = inside front cover; **tp** = title page; **cp** = contents page; **ap1** = acknowledgements page 1; **ap2** = acknowledgements page 2; **ibc** = inside back cover; **bc** = back cover; **3** = page 3; **4** = page 4; etc.

Key to object position on page

tl = top left; *t* = top; *tc* = top centre; *tr* = top right; *cla* = centre left above; *ca* = centre above; *cra* = centre right above; *cl* = centre left; *c* = centre; *cr* = centre right; *clb* = centre left below; *cb* = centre below; *crb* = centre right below; *bl* = bottom left; *b* = bottom; *bc* = bottom centre; *br* = bottom right; *w* = whole page; *h* = header; *tb* = text background

Key to image licence types

CC BY-SA 2.0 = https://creativecommons.org/licenses/by-sa/2.0/deed.en;

CC BY-SA 3.0 = https://creativecommons.org/licenses/by-sa/3.0/deed.en;

CC BY-SA 4.0 = https://creativecommons.org/licenses/by-sa/4.0/deed.en;

(m) = image has been modified as permitted under licensing terms

fc *br*: Errol Flynn (m) © Photoplay, Wikimedia Commons, CC BY-SA 4.0; **fc** *cla*: Franklin D. Roosevelt (m) © Leon Perskie / FDR Presidential Library & Museum, Wikimedia Commons, CC BY-SA 2.0; **4** *bl*: V-1 Bomb, © Tlford2035, Wikimedia Commons, CC BY-SA 4.0; **5** *bl*: Erwin Rommel, © Bundesarchiv, Bild 146-1977-018-13A/Otto, Wikimedia Commons, CC BY-SA 3.0; **18** *cla*: Rutger Hauer © DWDD, Wikimedia Commons, CC BY-SA 3.0; **18** *clb*: Alice Walker © Ms. magazine, Wikimedia Commons, CC BY-SA 4.0; **19** *cla*: Jerry Springer © Justin Hoch, Wikimedia Commons, CC BY-SA 2.0; **19** *clb*: Roger Daltrey © Jennifer Hammer, Wikimedia Commons, CC BY-SA 2.0; **20** *cla*: Dame Kiri Te Kanawa © New Zealand Government, Office of the Governor-General, Wikimedia Commons, CC BY-SA 4.0; **20** *clb*: Diana Ross © Raph_PH, Wikimedia Commons, CC BY-SA 2.0; **21** *cla*: Len Goodman © alotofmillion, Wikimedia Commons, CC BY-SA 3.0; **21** *clb*: George Lucas © nicolas genin, Wikimedia Commons, CC BY-SA 2.0; **22** *cla*: Ray Davies © ultomatt, Wikimedia Commons, CC BY-SA 2.0; **22** *clb*: Jeff Beck © Egghead06, Wikimedia Commons, CC BY-SA 4.0; **23** *cla*: Clive Lloyd © AlanM04, Wikimedia Commons, CC BY-SA 3.0; **24** *cla*: Jacqueline Bisset © Andrey Lunin, Wikimedia Commons, CC BY-SA 2.0; **24** *clb*: Michael Douglas © Georges Biard, Wikimedia Commons, CC BY-SA 3.0; **25** *cla*: Bernard Hill © Gemma Longman, Wikimedia Commons, CC BY-SA 2.0; **25** *clb row 1*: Jimmy Page © Avda, Wikimedia Commons, CC BY-SA 3.0; **25** *cb row 1*: Joe Frazier © John Mathew Smith & www.celebrity-photos.com, Wikimedia Commons, CC BY-SA 2.0; **25** *crb row 1*: Bobby Ball © SolomanMcKenzie, Wikimedia Commons, CC BY-SA 3.0; **25** *clb row 2*: Roger Lloyd-Pack © antiwarassembly, Wikimedia Commons, CC BY-SA 3.0; **25** *cb row 2*: Alan Parker © Lisa Moran Parker, Wikimedia Commons, CC BY-SA 1.0; **25** *crb row 2*: Sir Ranulph Fiennes © David Ward, Wikimedia Commons, CC BY-SA 3.0; **25** *clb row 3*: Pattie Boyd © Eddie Janssens, Wikimedia Commons, CC BY-SA 4.0; **25** *cb row 3*: Joe Cocker © Thesupermat, Wikimedia Commons, CC BY-SA 3.0; **25** *crb row 3*: Gladys Knight © Kingkongphoto & www.celebrity-photos.com, Wikimedia Commons, CC BY-SA 2.0; **25** *cb row 4*: John Simpson © Chatham House, Wikimedia Commons, CC BY-SA 2.0; **25** *crb row 4*: Angela Rippon © Number 10, Wikimedia Commons, CC BY-SA 2.0; **25** *clb row 5*: Tim Rice © Thecharmschool, Wikimedia Commons, CC BY-SA 4.0; **25** *cb row 5*: Danny DeVito © Gage Skidmore, Wikimedia Commons, CC BY-SA 3.0; **26** *clb*: Edvard Munch © Nasjonalbiblioteket, Wikimedia Commons, CC BY-SA 2.0; **27** *cl*: Erwin Rommel © Bundesarchiv, Bild 146-1977-018-13A/Otto, Wikimedia Commons, CC BY-SA 3.0; **29** *tl*: Coins © Jo Smiley Hailey, Unsplash.com; **29** *tr*: House © Sludgegulper, Wikimedia Commons, CC BY-SA 2.0; **29** *bl*: Radio © Auckland Museum, Wikimedia Commons, CC BY-SA 4.0; **29** *bc*: Bread © Dmitry Makeev, Wikimedia Commons, CC BY-SA 4.0; **29** *br*: Eggs © George Chernilevsky, Wikimedia Commons, CC BY-SA 4.0; **30** *tr*: Drilling Components © State Library of South Australia, Wikimedia Commons, CC BY-SA 2.0; **36** *ca*: Woolton Pie (m) © autumnroseuk, Wikimedia Commons, CC BY-SA 2.0; **37** *ca*: Carrot Cake (m) © Veganbaking.net from USA, Wikimedia Commons, CC BY-SA 2.0; **38** *cra*: Arthur's Seat (m) © Ad Meskens, Wikimedia Commons, CC BY-SA 3.0; **38** *crb*: Blackpool Tower (m) © Mike Peel, Wikimedia Commons, CC BY-SA 3.0; **44** *br*: The National Gallery (m) © Uukgoblin, Wikimedia Commons, CC BY-SA 3.0; **49** *cla*: Wynford Vaughan Thomas © BBC Photo Archive; **50** *cla*: Vera Lynn © Eric Koch / Anefo, Wikimedia Commons, CC BY-SA 3.0; **53** *clb*: The Royal Albert Hall © Diliff, Wikimedia Commons, CC BY-SA 3.0; **55** *tl*: Generative Art with the assistance of DALL·E 2; **55** *cl* & **55** *bl* & **56** *tl* & **56** *bl* & **57** *tl* & **57** *cl* & **57** *bl*: Generative Art with the assistance of Adobe Photoshop; **56** *cl*: Razor (m) © Dr.K, Wikimedia Commons, CC BY-SA 3.0; **56** *bl*: Temple (m) © Spenser Sembrat, Unsplash.com; **60** *clb*: Noele Gordon © The Noele Gordon Archive @ www.noelegordon.co.uk; **62** *cla*: Harvard Mark 1 (m) © Daderot, Wikimedia Commons, CC BY-SA 3.0; **63** *clb*: Sunset (m) © David Law, Unsplash.com; **68** *cra*: V-2 Rocket © AElfwine, Wikimedia Commons, CC BY-SA 3.0; **72** *tr*: Frank Jefferson © with thanks to Lancashire Fusiliers, www.lancs-fusiliers.co.uk; **73** *tl*: Medal of Freedom © Hdec, Wikimedia Commons, CC BY-SA 3.0; **73** *cla*: Legion of Honour Medal © Robert Lawton, Wikimedia Commons, CC BY-SA 2.5; **76** *clb*: Kofferset © Hanedoes, Wikimedia Commons, CC BY-SA 3.0; **77** *cl*: Tommy Harrisd © HM Government, Wikimedia Commons, OGL v1.0; **79** *cl*: Bomb Damaged conference room © Bundesarchiv, Bild 146-1972-025-10, Wikimedia Commons, CC BY-SA 3.0; **79** *br*: Hitler's damaged trousers © Bundesarchiv, Bild 146-1972-025-64, Wikimedia Commons ,CC BY-SA 3.0;

Photo Credits continued

Graphic and Background Image Credits

Credits shown in the order in which they appear in the book.

Additional Key

(ic) = icon; (ph) = photo

1944 : What A Year To Be Born!
Why not join our mailing list...

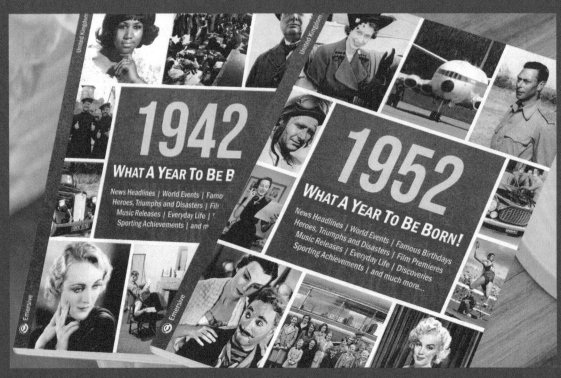

Join us for news on our future releases, reader promotions and behind-the-scenes content. All at:

www.subscribepage.com/whatayear

It's completely free to join. As a subscriber, we will email you no more than once or twice a month. We will never share your email address and you can unsubscribe at any time.

Key to Front Cover Images

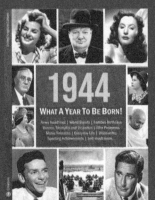

Clockwise from top left corner:
1. Actress Ingrid Bergman
2. Prime Minister Winston Churchill
3. Actress Barbara Stanwyck
4. Princess Elizabeth II
5. Mahatma Gandhi
6. Actor Errol Flynn
7. US troops landing on Omaha Beach on D-Day
8. Singer and actor Frank Sinatra
9. Her Majesty Queen Elizabeth
10. President Franklin D. Roosevelt

Made in the USA
Monee, IL
04 August 2024

63274225R00057